# Beowulf

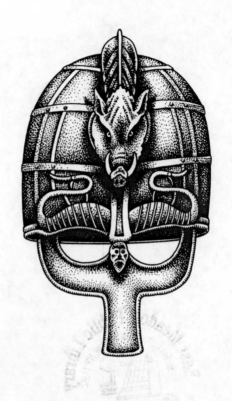

# BEOWULF
## An Imitative Translation
# BY RUTH P. M. LEHMANN

UNIVERSITY OF TEXAS PRESS

AUSTIN

Copyright © 1988
by the University of Texas Press
All rights reserved
Printed in the United States of America

Sixth paperback printing, 2000
Designed by George Lenox
Illustrations by Ed Lindlof

Requests for permission to reproduce material
from this work should be sent to
Permissions, University of Texas Press
Box 7819, Austin, Texas 78713-7819

∞

The paper used in this publication meets the
minimum requirements of American National
Standard for Information Sciences—Permanence
of Paper for Printed Library Materials, ANSI
Z39.48-1984.

Library of Congress
Cataloging-in-Publication Data

Beowulf, English.
    Beowulf: an imitative translation /
by Ruth P. M. Lehmann.—1st ed.
    p.    cm.
    Bibliography: p.
    Includes index.
    ISBN 978-0-292-70771-9
    1. Lehmann, Ruth, 1912–  II. Title.
PR1583.L38    1988
829'.3—dc19            88-10306

Dedicated to the memory of

DAVID DE CAMP

who urged me to undertake this translation
after reading my versions
of a few of the purple passages
of the original.

# CONTENTS

NETHERLANDS, NORTH GERMANY, AND SCANDINAVIA.
Tribes according to Klaeber's *Beowulf*.

# Introduction

THE UNIQUE MANUSCRIPT (ms.) Cotton Vitellus A. XV containing *Beowulf* is now in the British Library (formerly called the British Museum). The ms. was damaged in the fire at the Cotton Library, and although it is complete, parts of the ms. are very difficult. Two scribes penned this ms., the second beginning at line 1939 and continuing to the end. The Early English Texts Society has published a facsimile edition, and several excellent editions of the Old English text with useful introductions and notes have been produced; the most complete are those edited by Frederic Klaeber (Boston: D. C. Heath, 3d ed., 1950); C. L. Wrenn, fully revised by W. F. Bolton (London: Harrap, 1973); and Elliot van Kirk Dobbie, *Beowulf and Judith*, Anglo-Saxon Poetic Records (ASPR) IV (New York: Columbia University Press, 1953). All these have useful bibliographies. The arrangement is best in Wrenn, the rehearsal of suggestions and emendations by scholars fullest in ASPR, but Wrenn's edition is the most recent.

Dating of the poem is still under debate. The references in the preceding paragraph all have something to say about it, and dates from the sixth century to the early eleventh century (the date of the ms.) have been proposed. Only two very early linguistic forms occur and scholars have often edited these out. Those interested in linguistic questions must study the original poem. The note to line 1850 mentions the one early construction that affects the translation. Since in my own mind I must try to settle the question, I feel that eighth or ninth century consorts well with the language, the interest in Danish affairs, and the mixture of christian and Germanic virtues.

The tale, however, is not about times contemporary with the poet. The date of these intertribal quarrels is fifth century, a time of vessels made of hides stretched over a wooden frame and tarred for waterproofing. They were seaworthy, but best for coastal travel by sail or oars. Legend has it that one Irish hermit crossed to the New World, and a twentieth-century adventurer built such a ship and succeeded in making the same trip with it by using oars only to get beyond the coastal currents and then letting the ocean currents carry him north toward Iceland and then west toward Greenland. Those vessels were difficult to steer, for they had no keel and were hardly the "foamy-necked voyager" that the poet anachronistically introduced to take Beowulf south to Denmark. The poet describes the clinker-built Viking vessels that he knew, like that holding the ship-burial in the mound at Sutton Hoo, excavated just before the Second World War. The story of this discovery and the owner's gift of it to the British Library is told in detail in Rupert Bruce-Mitford's *Sutton Hoo Ship Burial*, 2d ed. (London: British Library, 1972); a two-volume version by Bruce-Mitford and others (same publisher, 1983); and *Aspects of Anglo-Saxon Archaeology: Sutton Hoo and Other Discoveries*, also by Bruce-Mitford (New York: Harper's Magazine Press and Harper and Row, 1974).

## THE POEM

*Scyldings Shelter Scyld.*   The poem begins with the legendary coming of Scyld as a baby set adrift alone in a boat and arriving on the Danish coast penniless. But when he grows up he becomes unifier, leader, and king of the Danes. On his death he is again set adrift, but now the boat is piled high with treasure and the standard floats in the wind on the mast above him. He leaves a son, Beow, already famous as a king in South Sweden (the northern part of Denmark in the fifth century). In the poem Scyld's son is called Beowulf, probably by confusion with the later hero, but for better meter and conforming to Norse genealogies, like some other translators I have used the traditional name.

*Danes, Danger, Daring.*   Beow carries on the Scylding line as a good and able ruler and is succeeded by his son Halfdane. Halfdane in turn is a worthy king, and has three sons—Heregar, Hrothgar, and Helga—and a daughter, Yrsa, who marries Onela of the royal line of Sweden. Halfdane is succeeded by his eldest son, Heregar, who leaves a son, Hereward, but he is passed over for the inheritance, and Halfdane's second son, Hrothgar, becomes king when Heregar dies. Hrothgar shares the throne with Hrothulf, son of Helga, the youngest brother. Hrothgar rules long and well.

With the kingdom stable, Hrothgar orders that a great banquet hall be built. Workmen from far and near are brought to build and decorate this royal building. Its fine workmanship and gilded gables are famous abroad as well as in Denmark. Hrothgar names the hall Heorot or Hart. (Tradition places it near Leire on Zealand, a few miles south of Roskilde.) The drinking, laughter, and carousing of the warriors as they relax of an evening provoke a savage monster named Grendel. Only gradually do we learn details of the creature, but later it takes four men to carry his head on a spear, and his arm ends in a paw with sharp claws like steel spikes. For weeks and months Grendel visits Hart Hall nightly, devouring sleeping warriors and carrying off others to the moor to feed on later. At last only after drunken boasting to guard the stronghold does anyone linger in the hall after dark.

News of Hrothgar's assailant travels eventually to other lands, and Beowulf, sister's son to Hygelac, King of the Geats, with somewhat grudging consent from his uncle, sails with chosen companions from southwestern Sweden on the east coast of the Oslofjord. When the coastal watchman learns that they have come to Hrothgar's aid, he shows them the path to Hart. The Geats set out in marching order.

At Hart the Geats enter with greetings and courtesies on both sides that show the observation of etiquette in the court. King Hrothgar had earlier given protection to Beowulf's father, Ecgtheow, when the Swedes did not wish to get involved in his blood-feud with an eastern Germanic tribe that he had offended. Hearing Beowulf's name, Hrothgar recalls hearing of the extraordinary strength and fine reputation of the Geatish hero. The Geats are warmly received and Beowulf is seated on the bench with Hrothgar's young sons. No Dane has confronted Grendel successfully. But the enthusiastic welcome to the Geats angers Unferth, Hrothgar's official spokesman. He taunts Beowulf for having been defeated in a swimming contest with Breca.

Beowulf sets the record straight by recounting the dangers— attacking sea-monsters, storms, vast distances—and claiming that they had merely arranged a kind of boyish hunt for sea-beasts. Separated by the storm, they swam different paths; Breca to Romerike in Norway, Beowulf to the land of Finns. Beowulf ends his retort with a taunt that Unferth has slain his own brother, the ultimate crime, even by accident. At nightfall Hrothgar and all the Danes leave Hart Hall to sleep elsewhere, leaving Beowulf and the Geats to occupy the hall benches, risking their lives.

As darkness descends Grendel comes trudging toward Heorot and pushes wide the doors with his huge paw. He lays hold and munches down the nearest warrior. Beowulf has vowed to use no weapon, since Grendel uses none. Later the Geats learn that Grendel has put a spell on all weapons so that none can harm him. Next he reaches for Beowulf, but the hero grasps his arm and rises to his feet. In the ferocious struggle that follows, the hero wrenches off the monster's arm. The sounds of the combat terrify the Danes outside: Grendel howling with pain, tables and benches torn up and overturned, Hart shaken to its foundations. Grendel, leaving a trail of blood, struggles back to the mere and dies. Beowulf fixes his arm high above the hall at the gable-end.

Hrothgar and all the Danes gather in the hall to admire the hairy paw and its vicious claws. Then, after following the bloody spoor to the mere they return in high spirits, composing a song of Beowulf's adventure. They tell also of the dragon-slaying of Sigemund and his nephew Fitela. The warriors race their horses and return rejoicing to Hart.

They come back to a banquet of celebration. After the feast a bard sings the story of Finnsburg and the sorrow of Hildeburh. (The early part of this feud is told in the Finnsburg Fragment, given after the poem of Beowulf.) In this story, we learn of the deaths of Hnaef and his sister's son, then in the renewed battle, the death of Finn, Hildeburh's husband. The banquet ends with most generous gift-giving by Hrothgar to Beowulf. Then Hrothgar and Wealhtheow, his queen, go to their room apart, and Beowulf, too, is favored by a room elsewhere, while the Danes at last dare to sleep in the hall.

*Monster-Mother of the Mere.* During the night Grendel's grieving mother comes from the mere, snatches a sleeping Dane, then, spotting the arm, jerks it from the wall and carries that and the dead warrior back to the mere. In the morning Hrothgar is again plunged in sorrow. An honored leader, Ashhere, is dead. Unfortunately the Geats have been given benches less exposed to intruders.

When Beowulf hears of the new trouble, he again offers his help. Hrothgar tells him of a mysterious land not far away, where two strange creatures have been seen, one a huge male, the other a female. Unferth presents his heirloom sword, Hrunting, to

Beowulf to use against this new foe. The king mounts his horse and conducts the Geats to the edge of a pool. When Beowulf leaves, he asks that the gifts he received the night before be sent to Hygelac, King of the Geats, if he himself never returns. Hrothgar and some of his men return to Hart; the rest and the Geats settle down to wait while their leader plunges into the pool.

Grendel's mother realizes someone is invading the mere and grasps Beowulf. He is attacked on all sides by submarine creatures, but his armor protects him as the sea-monster carries him down to the depths. He finds himself at last in a vaulted hall where the water cannot reach and a fire burns in the depths beyond. When he deals the creature a blow with Hrunting, the sword will not bite, and he tosses it aside and grabs her. But she upsets him and sits on top of him, trying to cut through his armor with her knife. Beowulf sees a giant sword on the wall, tosses her off and seizes it. With a powerful blow he decapitates her.

The fire flares up and he sees Grendel lying dead. He cuts off his head with the giant sword, and Grendel's hot blood melts all the sword-blade but the hilt. With the hilt, Hrunting, and Grendel's head Beowulf swims back to the surface. Meanwhile the Danes had seen Grendel's and his mother's blood discolor the water and, sure of the worst, had returned to Hart. But the Geats are all there to meet their chief on his return. They help him—four carrying Grendel's head—bring the spoils back to Hrothgar's court.

Beowulf tells briefly his adventure in the heart of the mere, mentions that Hrunting did not avail him, and tells how he saw the wondrous sword hanging on the wall and with it slew the great trolls. He presents the hilt to Hrothgar, who reads on it the runes telling of Noah's flood and the name of him for whom the sword had been made. In his acceptance speech Hrothgar praises Beowulf but warns him against becoming too self-confident and arrogant. An early Danish king, Heremod, is an example of how one greatly favored by God may become a selfish and violent ruler. Parsimony is the unforgivable sin of a ruler. Hrothgar presses this point in a lengthy sermon, a poor reward to a hero who has twice risked his life where no Dane would go to rescue these foreigners. Hrothgar concludes by promising to reward Beowulf in the morning.

A feast follows, but they retire soon after. In the morning Beowulf returns Hrunting to Unferth, thanking him but with great tact saying nothing of its having failed him. The Geats are now restless so the hero says farewell and they return to the sea-coast where their ship rides at anchor. He offers further support to the Danes if ever they should need it, but Hrothgar takes a tearful farewell.

Happy with the treasure Hrothgar has donated, the Geats return to Hygelac. Once in his presence Beowulf gives him all that he has received, including the heirloom sword of Heregar that had been denied his son Hereward. To Hygd, the young queen, he gives the Brosings' necklace, gift of Wealhtheow. Hygelac matches the gifts with money and lands. Hygd is especially commended as not like Thryth in arrogance toward her suitors before she followed her father's counsel and crossed the sea to marry Offa.

Beowulf's account of his adventures in Denmark tells a number of details that had not been revealed before. Handscioh is the name of the Geat killed by Grendel before Beowulf laid a hand on him. The monster was equipped with a large pouch in which he stuffed the victims he did not devour on the spot. Then Beowulf foretells the fate of Hrothgar's daughter, not perhaps Wealhtheow's daughter, for her sons were younger and she pleaded with Hrothulf to treat them fairly. This story, like that of Finnsburg, was doubtless well known to the poem's audience. It is another of a young bride, Freawaru, married off to patch up a feud. But the old hard feelings are easily wakened and Ingeld falls out of love with Freawaru through no fault of hers.

*The Dragon and Death.*   Transitional matter is disposed of in a few lines. Hygelac is killed on the continent, fighting the Franks. Hygd asks Beowulf to become king and protect her young son Heardred. Beowulf refuses the rank, but promises to protect Heardred and lead the army for him until he is old enough to take command. Heardred as king gives refuge to the sons of Ohthere, who have rebelled against their uncle, Onela, King of Sweden. The Geat is killed in an engagement that arose from these Geatish wars with the Swedes. Thereupon Beowulf becomes king (and possibly marries Hygd).

A digression tells how the last survivor of an ancient race buried their treasures in a cavern. Long after, a dragon (wyrm) finds it and becomes its self-appointed guardian. Beowulf comes to the throne and rules for fifty years. During his last years as an old king a slave of one of his vassal lords discovers the cavern and investigates, finding the treasure and the sleeping dragon. He steals a rich cup to placate his master and brings the cup to his lord. The dragon wakes, realizes the hoard has been plundered, and then nightly flies about with its fiery breath burning stronghold, village, and countryside. Beowulf says it is his duty alone to bring peace. First, knowing no other way to face the blaze, he has an iron shield made to protect him from the flames.

By this time the cup has been turned over to the king. Beowulf takes eleven picked men with him, and the terrified thief—the thirteenth man—to show the way. Leaving his men at the entrance, he challenges the dragon with a mighty shout and enters the cavern to face it. In the ensuing combat, though his shield gives him some protection, the claws and jaws of the wyrm and its flames stronger than ever are overwhelming him. His men take to the woods, all but his kinsman, Wiglaf, a Swede referred to as prince of the Scylfings. Beowulf has had forebodings about this fight, and now his blow is weaker than he had hoped. Wiglaf urges the others of the troop to go with him to aid the king, but in vain.

The dragon makes a second attack, but Wiglaf dashes in to the shelter of Beowulf's shield. Beowulf strikes with his own sword, Naegling, but it shatters. At the third assault the dragon grasps Beowulf's neck in its poisonous jaws. Wiglaf strikes for the underbelly. Meanwhile Beowulf draws his dagger and slashes the wyrm open in the middle. The fire begins to subside; the two kinsmen together have killed the dragon.

But the bite was venomous. Exhausted and in pain Beowulf sits on a stone ledge while Wiglaf bathes him with water to revive him. The king asks him to bring some of the treasure that he may gauge its value. Wiglaf hastens farther into the cave and brings back an armload of precious heirlooms and a banner woven of golden thread. But on his return his king is near death. He sprinkles him with water and he rouses briefly, asking that they raise his tomb on Whale's Cape. Then he dies.

The other ten slink into the cave. Wiglaf lectures them on the duty of thanes to their lord in payment for the arms he gives them. Then they push the dragon over the cliff onto the rocks below and prepare the funeral pyre and the barrow on the headland.

The treasure is buried below the tomb, forever useless as before. A solemn procession of thanes tells Beowulf's glorious deeds and a Geatish woman croons a lament. In the final summing up it is not his strength and courage that they laud, but his kindness, thoughtfulness, and hope to be remembered with praise.

## THE EARLY GERMANIC BACKGROUND

Although Beowulf does not appear in any of the Norse chronicles and it is to be guessed that he and the mythical monsters he encounters are fiction, yet the poem presents a world foreign to us, but very much that of the early middle ages when it was written. On the one hand we have references to old legends of the sorrows of Hildeburh, Ingeld and his wife Freawaru, Sigemund and Fitela, and the troubled wars of the Geats and Swedes, the Danish royal line, a glance at the taming of Thryth, and olden customs and assumptions. Because so much knowledge is assumed, perhaps some explanation at least of the important sense of values and motivations of those days of old can point the direction of further investigation and greater understanding.

Even commonplace matters—the kind of warfare and weapons, the differences between that world and the more recent Arthurian period—need clarification. The watchman at the coast has a horse so that he can oversee greater distances and get back to his lord before an intruder—friendly or hostile—invades his presence. Moreover, Hrothgar, an old king, rides to the mere to show Beowulf the way. All the fighting is done on foot. Armor is light to be a protection, not an incumbrance. The great hairy-footed destriers of the knights of Camelot had not yet been bred. Rather those who rode went on the plump, sturdy ponies of present Norway and Wales. Armor was either linked chain-mail or heavy leather studded with metal, reinforced with metal discs or rings, but surely no plate armor of the fourteenth and fifteenth centuries.

Spears or javelins were mainly for throwing, not the heavy rigid lances that the Arthurian knights used to poke each other from their steeds. Bows and arrows were used by trained bowmen. The art of fletching (mounting feathers on an arrow so that it would spiral in a straighter line) took special training. But the smiths were the most honored of the class of armorers, since they forged the great two-handed falchions, the claymores of the Celts, that we know most recently in the great weapons used for the execution of criminals in the fifteenth century. Often these were old, taken from a vanquished enemy or the gift of a lord to a vassal for unusual distinction in combat. They were heavy and awkward in a close encounter. Shorter one-handed weapons and daggers were better to manipulate except by the strongest and most experienced of warriors.

Although there was none of the ritual of vigil, vows, and prayers as for the knights of later centuries, there was a formal pledge to one's lord. In return the soldier was given his equipment for carrying out his duties. Wiglaf taunts the other members of Beowulf's picked troop of eleven who do not come to the king's aid against the dragon. Beowulf had given them their swords and armor; they offer him no return. Plundering the dead and defeated could also bring in equipment. It is recognition of some such sword of his father on an alien hip that causes the feud to break out between Ingeld's Heathobards and the Danes and leads eventually to the burning of Hart Hall (lines 81–85; the son-in-law is Ingeld, to whom Hrothulf betrays his uncle's banquet hall; see also lines 2022–2069). Since plunder and gifts were presented to the chief, as Beowulf gives those from Hrothgar to Hygelac, these were not only passed along to new members of the household, but also became part of the tribal hoard, like that the dragon presides over.

The treasures buried in the royal cenotaph (an empty tomb without a body) at Sutton Hoo contained shield ornaments, a sword, and a helmet that showed Swedish workmanship or Swedish design (see Bruce-Mitford, "The Swedish Connection," Chapter X of the 1983 edition of *Sutton Hoo Ship Burial*, and Mitford's *Aspects of Anglo-Saxon Archaeology*, pp. 47–52). Although *Beowulf* is an English poem in a mixture of dialects, it shows no Swedish influence in the telling. Yet the hero's father was Swedish, although he marries the Geatish King Hrethel's daughter, as Hrothgar the Dane's sister is married off to the Swedish prince Onela, both princesses probably to cement friendship between warring nations. Of course any connection between the fictional adventures of Beowulf and a real king's cenotaph at Sutton Hoo is not to be assumed. But the mixture of treasure can lead to speculation that the closeness of various Germanic tribes was a reality in the view the poet gives us of his own world. The burial was early in the seventh century; one scholar has dated the poem from the late seventh and another places it contemporary with the manuscript, three centuries later. Archaeologists do not fully agree that the mound at Sutton Hoo was a cenotaph, but in any case the grave objects are a mixture of christian and pagan, just as the poet realizes that the Danes were still pagan, yet Hrothgar's counsel is compatible with the christian ethic. Usually Rædwall is thought to be the king honored, for he was the first East Anglian ruler to be converted, though his wife remained pagan and later he joined her in pagan worship. The burials of Scyld and of Beowulf are pagan in details, although by the eight century England had accepted christianity.

Bowmen were called in when a village or fortress was under siege, but bows were not part of the equipment of the lord's special troop. This group is often called the "comitatus," a Latin term for English *duguþ*, one of the Old English words lost with what it designated. The adjective "doughty" is all that remains. These were the best and most trusted of the men around the lord. Beowulf is the most trusted of Hygelac's "duguth," Wiglaf of Beowulf's.

"The enemy" is an important part of war. As in Northern Ireland today and in the Near East, as well as in many other parts of the world, the foe was not a stranger of vastly different culture, but very often a neighboring tribe. We are used to hearing that all we need is a common language or knowledge of each other's languages to come to an understanding, but there is no evidence that even the more widely separated Germanic tribes like the Danes and Heathobards had difficulty communicating with each other. Danish and Norwegian—and with only a little more difficulty, Swedish and Danish—are mutually understandable. The political divisions do not divide the cultures. Moreover, frequent intermarriages kept the bonds close.

Even more of a problem for us is understanding the role of women and what their lives were really like.

## A WOMAN'S PLACE

A woman was always under the authority of a man. At the same time, he was responsible and some women made a great deal of trouble for their husbands by promoting feuds, running up debts, even instigating the servants to steal for them. But in *Beowulf* the women are mere pawns in a man's chess game. A woman's freedom was very likely in the domestic sphere where she had her handiwork, her female companions, her decisions, and her responsibilities. Perhaps by comparison with some strict, secluded religious groups like the Catholic orders, the Moslems, and some of the strict Protestant groups like the Amish we can grasp what the women's satisfactions were in spite of their restrictions.

*Beowulf* tells of rebellious Thryth, harsh toward her suitors and apparently indulged by her father until King Offa fell in love with her and made her happy, but only after she did as her father wished. The other women in the poem are married off as "peace-weavers" to strengthen the temporary friendship of formerly hostile tribes. Wealhtheow may have been such a one, although the peace is broken outside the poem and merely hinted at in the tale. Even then the quarrel is not directly because of her, but she is a Helming from an East Germanic tribe from Pomerania, a Wylfing, like the warrior that Ecgtheow had slain, and from that same general area came the Heathobards. Hrothgar has married off his daughter to Ingeld, a Heathobard, to bring peace, but these rise up and storm Hart. Hrothgar's associate, Hrothulf, son of Helga, betrays Hart to Ingeld, and Wealhtheow's sons are killed, in spite of her earlier pleas to Hrothulf after the banquet for Beowulf's ridding Hart of Grendel and his mother.

The only duty we see a lady undertake is distributing mead, wine, or ale to her husband and his visitors. There was doubtless etiquette in the serving depending on where one sat. The ladies would offer superior drinks to their lord, his special guests, or the hero of the moment and possibly his family. Ale, perhaps sweetened with honey (you can still try it at the old capital of Sweden at Gamla Uppsala from one of their special goblets), then plain ale and beer to the warriors of less prestige than the duguth. Drunkenness was not frowned on. "Flushed with wine" is a frequent epithet in the tales and songs, but often in connection with foolish boasting or daring.

## HISTORICAL BACKGROUND

Perhaps you have already noted that the names given sons alliterate with their father's name in many of the western Germanic tribes. The Danes after Halfdane were Heregar, Hrothgar, and Helga. Helga's son was Hrothulf, Heregar's son Hereward. Another branch had Hoc, father of Hnaef and Hildeburh, but hers is the only woman's name that so alliterates. Hrothgar's sister is Yrsa, his daughter Freawaru. The Swedish royal line alliterated: Ongentheow, Ohthere, Onela; the next generation Eanmund and Eadgils. But Wiglaf is called "prince of the Scylfings" and his name does not alliterate with the others but with that of his father, Wihstan. The name of his kinsman Beowulf does not alliterate but is possibly a nickname—the bee-wolf, or bear—recalling his prodigious strength. In contrast note the names of the eastern Germanic Heathobards: Ingeld, son of Froda. This naming convention was surely useful to the poets composing verses praising a man and his ancestors, and we, too, can make use of it as a mnemonic to keep straight some of these relationships. Beowulf's father was Ecgtheow, a Swede; was he of the royal line? Some scholars have wondered if Beowulf may not be the nickname of Alfhere, unidentified, but mentioned as kinsman of Wiglaf.

What we know with more certainty is discussed in the introductions, notes, and appendices of the editions of the poem mentioned earlier, as well as in commentaries on the poem. Two excellent ones are R. W. Chambers, *Beowulf: An Introduction to the Study of the Poem with a Discussion of Offa and Finn*, 3d ed. (Cambridge: Cambridge University Press, 1963); and G. N. Garmonsway and Jacqueline Simpson, *Beowulf and Its Analogues* (London: J. M. Dent and Sons; New York: E. P. Dutton and Co., 1968). In this latter volume, the analogues are all translated as well as the poem. One further commentary gives an excellent account of some themes and the geography of the underwater cave: W. W. Lawrence, *Beowulf and Epic Tradition* (Cambridge, Mass.: Harvard Press, 1930). More recent but based on speculation rather than certainties is Edward B. Irving, Jr., *A Reading of Beowulf* (New Haven and London: Yale University Press, 1968). Irving is a sensitive reader and his hunches are interesting, even when not compelling.

The historical sources are chiefly Scandinavian, presenting a world similar to that of the poem with many tribes associated by marriage and geography, for the most part following the same or similar customs. It was a pagan world, unlike England of the eighth or ninth centuries, which was largely christian. Just how christian the poem and its spirit are has been debated. For a variety of facets of this matter, see the essays (especially the one by

C. L. Wrenn) in L. E. Nicholson, ed., *An Anthology of Beowulf Criticism* (Notre Dame, Ind.: University of Notre Dame Press, 1963), and Bernard F. Huppé, *The Hero in the Earthly City: A Reading of Beowulf* (Binghamton: Medieval and Renaissance Texts and Studies, SUNY, Binghamton, 1984 [with translation]). Other topics that are of interest are also discussed in Nicholson's collection. It has been pointed out that only Old Testament characters and stories are referred to and the poet sees no conflict between christian and old Germanic values. Funerals of Scyld, Hnaef, and Beowulf follow pagan customs. The hero wishes praise after death from men, not permission to enter the Pearly Gates. None of the rituals of christianity is imposed on any characters, and once in a while the poet remembers that they worshipped at heathen altars.

Close family ties in Norse story led to two customs. One is the importance of the sister's son, who is sent to fosterage in his mother's family. The daughter of a household was often given in marriage to a warrior as a reward for outstanding service (Hygelac's daughter to Eofor for killing Ongentheow, the Swedish king), or more regularly—as pointed out in the discussion of women's place above—to a hostile tribe to fix a peace-bond (Hildeburh to Finn, Freawaru to Ingeld, probably Wealhtheow to Hrothgar, Hrethel's daughter to Ecgtheow, and Yrsa to Onela.) Neither Wealhtheow nor Yrsa sends her children back to her family in the poem.

The second consequence of strong family feelings and coolness toward other tribes in Norse accounts is incest. From such unions comes the perfect hero with courage, strength, and all the "right stuff." In Norse stories Hrothulf's mother is Yrsa, sister of Helga, his father. Helga and Hrothulf are the great warriors and Hrothgar is a weakling. In the Norse version of the Sigemund story, Fitela is his son by his sister, who deliberately enters into the relationship in order to bear a son who can take vengeance on her husband. In Germany incest also appears in the story of Siegfried.

But the Anglo-Saxons took a different view. In tales from the twelfth to the fifteenth centuries King Arthur's incest occurs unwittingly, at least on his part, and the child, Mordred, is a dark, treacherous figure who brings the end of Camelot. In *Beowulf* Hrothulf is called "brother's son," *suhterga*, for Old English had many specific words for relationships that the later language has lost.

The tensions of the poem stem from sibling rivalry and resentment of slights. Hrethel takes in Beowulf, his daughter's son, when he is only seven. (Her brothers are not eligible to do so; they are perhaps quite a bit younger than she, for Beowulf seems little younger than the youngest, Hygelac.) Hrethel treats his grandson like one of his sons (lines 2429–2434), but the young Geats, probably Hrethel's elder sons, Herebald and Hathcyn, might well have thought of their nephew as a potential rival and called him lazy and unpromising (lines 2183–2188). The rivalries in Hrothgar's house are even clearer, although many scholars have admired him as the nearly perfect king. He says of his older brother, Heregar, "He was better than I," but he denies his nephew, Hereward, his right, in contrast to Beowulf, who refuses the throne when Hygd offers it but guards the country until Hygd's son is of age. Heregar's splendid sword Hrothgar gives to Beowulf, not to the son, Hereward. Hrothgar's fellow ruler is not Heregar's son, but Hrothulf, Helga's son. The outcome is only hinted at in the poem but explicit in some of the Norse versions: Hrothulf betrays Hart to the Heathobards and the stronghold is burned. But eventually Hereward shows his mettle and wins the Danish throne after slaying his cousin.

More has been said of the Danes than of other tribes, for Hrothgar and his court are defended in two of Beowulf's contests. But when the scene changes to the Geats and Swedes, other peoples become important. The Geats are the Hrethlings, descendants and followers of Hrethel. Herebald, his eldest son, is accidentally killed when his younger brother, Hathcyn, shoots amiss at a target. Hrethel dies of grief soon after, and Hygelac, the youngest son, succeeds, with Beowulf, his sister's son, as chief warrior.

The poem tells us little of campaigns and battles, but in a skirmish between the Swedes and Geats the Swedish king, Ongentheow, kills Hathcyn. This takes place before Beowulf goes to Denmark, but the chronology of the action is not clear in the poem. After Beowulf's return Hygelac undertakes his fatal expedition to the continent and Beowulf guards the Geats until Heardred assumes the kingship. Heardred offers shelter to Eanmund and Eadgils, Ohthere's sons who rebel against Onela, who, if the younger brother, would be a usurper, like Hrothgar who denies Hereward his birthright. It should be noted, however, that not primogeniture, but rather a pledge of loyalty from the duguth, determined the succession. By talking down Hereward's qualifications, Hrothgar could justify his action.

Heardred's support of the rebellious brothers is disastrous. Wihstan, whom we meet later as father of Wiglaf and relative of Beowulf, a Swede like Ecgtheow and loyal to Onela, kills the older of Ohthere's sons, Eanmund. Heardred, too, is cut down in one of the skirmishes with the Swedes. In other texts we learn that the second brother, Eadgils, eventually kills his uncle, Onela, and claims the Swedish throne himself.

We hear nothing of Beowulf's involvement in the actions that led to the death of his uncle and king, Hygelac, though he does slay Dayraven who killed him. Nor do we hear of him in the Swedish wars when Heardred is slain. Now, however, he becomes king of the Geats and lives as a distinguished ruler for "fifty years." Was it that Beowulf with a Swedish father had conflicting loyalties? The poet, too, seems sympathetic to the old king Ongentheow, bravely defending himself against the young Geat brothers, Wulf and Eofor. The old king badly wounds Wulf, but Eofor strikes him down, and Hygelac honors his warrior with his daughter as bride.

So much for what we can glean from historical documents.

## THE FABULOUS

Parallels with a number of folktales and some of the sagas suggest the background of Beowulf's battles in Denmark and Geatland. These analogues are given in the sources cited. But the structure of this "main action" of the poem deserves comment. Grendel is Beowulf's most easily destroyed opponent. They fight without shields or weapons, and it is as much Grendel's eagerness to get away as Beowulf's strength that pulls off his arm so that he bleeds to death in his underwater home.

Although before the encounter with Grendel's mother the poet says the hero was as much less troubled as a woman's strength is less than a man's, yet he takes his armor and Unferth's sword, Hrunting, when he dives into the pool. In the struggle she trips Beowulf, he falls, and she sits on him, trying to cut through his armor with her knife. But of course the hero is able to toss her aside and regain his footing. When he strikes her, Hrunting fails him, but he sees a magic sword on the wall (perhaps the motif of the monster to be killed only by its own weapon) and decapitates her. Not her blood but Grendel's when Beowulf takes his head as a trophy melts the swordblade. The hero is victor, but hardly as easily as when he tore the arm from the son.

In the final fight with the dragon Beowulf has misgivings as to the outcome. He refuses to ask for help, though he does have a special metal shield made to ward off the dragon's hot breath. His blow is weaker than of old, but his young relative, Wiglaf, rushes in and by stabbing the dragon on its underbelly helps Beowulf to destroy it. Yet the dragon's venom kills the hero shortly after. This then is the hardest battle of all.

But consider the three adversaries. The least formidable was Grendel, a monster angered by the joy of others, greedy, brutal, laughing at the slaughter and devastation he brought on Hrothgar. His mother, however, comes for vengeance, her heart heavy at the loss of her son, lonely in her empty lair. Finally the dragon has stumbled on an unguarded hoard, buried long ago in a rocky cavern. Knowing the duty of dragons, it coils itself about the gold to protect it. After many years a thief finds the entrance, steals inside, and carries off a rich cup. On waking, the wyrm senses the violation and flies off on nightly excursions, burning crops and villages with its blazing breath and even demolishing the Geats' stronghold. Beowulf is doing his duty as king when he attacks it; the dragon is doing its duty as a dragon when it retaliates. The only lawbreaker is the thief.

## THE TRANSLATION

The translation is more or less imitative of Germanic alliterative verse. A more exact imitation is compromised by an effort not to distort modern English into something awkward and unintelligible. English has changed much since the Norman Conquest; the changes filled the language with French and latinate vocabulary, often with accompanying loss of the old Germanic words. Articles developed only later, pronoun subjects cannot now be omitted, the word order has become fixed, and these changes are as much for grammaticality as for intelligibility. On the other hand inflectional endings have been lost or reduced so far that the most frequent rhythm of Old English—ending on an unstressed syllable—has given way to the iambic rhythm of the modern language.

To be accurate in interpretation and keep to the alliterative meter I have here and there used uncommon words, but except for a few—*wyrd* for "fate" or "Providence," *wyrm* for "dragon"— the terms can be found in any Collegiate Desk Dictionary. Also a few of the possibilities of Old English appear here: "hand and hard sword" shows the alliteration of a preceding adjective, rather than the noun; some negative adjectives like "unknown" may alliterate on the vowel or N; but finite verbs, regularly unstressed in Old English, may or may not be stressed, for they are differently placed in the older language. Loss of inflectional syllables is somewhat compensated for by using particles that follow a verb as a drop (unstressed syllable), as in phrases like "tell it," "try to."

The discussion now becomes even more technical. Only students of Old English might find some profit in it.

Eduard Sievers is the German scholar who examined alliterative verse to determine the acceptable patterns. Although his scheme suggests only four syllables in the half-line, or verse, that is for the most part the minimum length. But there is no need here to give more exact rules. In the list below the letters indicate the frequency of each type of verse: *A* the most frequent, etc. Major stresses are marked /, secondary \, the drop X; the first half-line is called the on-verse, the second the off-verse. *A:* /X/X; *B:* X/X/; *C:* X//X; *D₁:* //\X; *D₂:* //X\; *E:* /\X/.

To accommodate the modern tendency to use articles, this version has more lines than the original showing anacrusis in types A, D, and even E (where it was avoided), but in these types I have tried to limit anacrusis to a single syllable, though it may not be the kind of particle occurring in Old English anacrusis.

Alliteration counts only on stressed syllables: moRose, reWard, perMit (verb), Permit (noun). As in Old English SP-, ST-, SK- alliterate only with themselves. In names HR- alliterates on R (Hrothgar), HN- on N (Hnaef), WR- on R (wrong), and Hygelac is pronounced "Heelac," Heremond "Haremund," Sigemund "Seamund." Modern words that may be pronounced differently as the speed of utterance differs (wanderer or wand'rer, reveling or rev'ling, heaven or heav'n, foreigner or for'ner) may be pronounced as fits the meter. Geat alliterates on Y and probably would be pronounced, had it survived, to rime with either "mates" or "meets" (like the poets Yeats or Keats). Scyld Scefing should be pronounced "shilled shaving." Of modern words, "one," if stressed, alliterates on W. In short, sound not letter determines the alliteration.

Some verses here are set out some spaces toward the left margin. These are the hypermetric lines, and in a number of early poems, as in *Beowulf* (lines 1162–1168, 1705–1707, 2994–2995), they occur in clusters of varying lengths. These lines have in part a regular pattern of one of Sievers' five types, but to the on-verses a third, non-alliterating lift and drop or drop and lift is added. This additional stress follows the regular type in the on-verse, but is prefixed to it in the off-verse.

1705  ðin ofer þēoda gehwylce.  Eal þū hit geþyldum healdest,
      mægen mid mōdes snyttrum.  Ic þē sceal mīne gelæstan
      frēode, swā wit furðum sprǣcon.

                        Ðū scealt tō frōfre
                        weorþan

1705  even over every nation.  You managed all your power
      with patience and prudence of spirit.  As I had proffered
                        before now,
      I shall fulfill our friendship.
                      "You shall be a future comfort,

For a concise summary of Sievers' study of metrics, see any edition of Bright's *Old English Grammar and Reader*. The most recent is that by Frederick Cassidy and his colleague Richard Ringler (New York: Holt, Rinehart and Winston, 1971). Although there are other studies and theories, they are for students of Old English.

As a sample of the original, here is the last part of what is known as "The Lay of the Last Survivor." This is the warrior of an ancient race who buried the dragon's hoard (lines 2258–2266).

gē swylce sēo herepād,  sīo æt hilde gebād
ofer borda gebræc  bite īrena,
brosnað æfter beorne;  ne mæg byrnan hring
æfter wīgfruman  wīde fēran
hæleðum be healfe.  Næs hearpan wyn,
gomen glēobēames,  nē gōd hafoc
geond sæl swingeð,  nē se swifta mearh
burhstede bēateð.  Bealocwealm hafað
fela feorhcynna  forð onsended!

# BEOWULF
## An Imitative Translation

# The Dane's Story:
## SCYLDINGS SHELTER SCYLD

NOW WE HAVE HEARD STORIES of high valor
in times long past    of tribal monarchs,
lords of Denmark,    how those leaders strove.
      Often Scyld Scefing    by the shock of war
5   kept both troops and tribes    from treasured meadbench,
filled foes with dread    after first being
discovered uncared for;    a cure for that followed:
he grew hale under heaven,    high in honor,
until no nation    near the borders,
10  beyond teeming seas    but was taught to obey,
giving tribute.    He was a good ruler.
      To him a boy was born,    a baby in the homestead,
whom God grants us    as gift and comfort
to ease the people.    He apprehended
15  dire trouble dogged    those destitute people.
But the Lord of life,    Leader of heaven,
offered them honor,    earthly requital.
Beow* was famous—    abroad well renowned—
throughout south Sweden*,    the successor to Scyld.
20  Thus should a fine young man    on his father's throne
give generously,    and do good to all
so that when aging,    old companions
stand by him steady    at the stroke of war,
his people serve him.    By praiseworthy deeds
25  each must prosper    in every tribe.
      Scyld passed away,    shut off as fated,
forth-faring strong,    to his Father's hands.
To the ocean current    then his own comrades
bore him among them,    as he had bidden them
30  while their loved leader,    lord of Scyldings,
yet might rule his speech;    his reign had been lengthy.
      There at the harbor stood    the high-beaked vessel,
ice-marked and eager,    their own king's transport.

[ 21 ]

Then they laid him down,   their loved chieftain,
35   ring-renderer,   to rest amidships,
their master by the mastfoot.   Many a treasure
from distant countries,   adornments, were laid there.
I heard of no comelier   keel made ready
with war weapons   and weeds of battle,
40   bills and breastmail.   On his breast there lay
piled in plenty   portioned treasure
that would fare afar   in the flood's embrace.
Not at all less they allowed   of allotted treasure,
of princely riches,   than those people did
45   who at time's threshold   turned forth alone
that little baby   on that lone journey.
There a standard stood,   streaming golden,
high overhead.   They let the heaving sea
bear him on the billows.   They had brooding thoughts,
50   mournful spirits.   Those men could not
tell indeed truly,   though they gave trusted advice,
that warriors over waters   welcomed that burden.

# Grendel's Coming:
## DANES, DANGER, DARING

Then in boroughs and towns   Beow, the Scylding,
belovèd leader,   through a long kingship
55 was most famed to his folk   (his father had departed,
high prince from his homeland),   until Halfdane, the Tall,
had been reared to rule.   He reigned to his deathday,
agèd, but able,   among his own people.
To the battle-prince   were born on earth
60 Four fine children,   forth numbered here:
Heregar, Hrothgar,   and Helga, the Good.
I heard that [Yrsa]   was Onela's queen,*
The Battle-Scylfing's   bridal consort.
     Then Hrothgar rose   to rank and honor,
65 warfare's rewards.   Well they obeyed him,
friendly followers,   until the force of youths
became a mighty band.   It came to his mind later
to make a meadhall,   put his men to work
on a hall higher,   handsomer, too,
70 then yet any man   had ever heard of.
He offered inside   to both old and young
goods God bestowed,   but not gifts breaking
public holdings,   nor of people's lives.
Then I widely heard   work demanded
75 of no few of the folk   throughout far countries
to beautify the building.   At the best moment
quickly among the people   it came to be ready,
of halls the greatest,   Hart, the name given
by him whose word held sway,   wide influence.
80 He kept his pledged promise,   portioned the rings,
favors at feasting.   The fair hall towered,
high, horn-gabled,   waiting hosts at war,
loathed lap of flames.   It was not long then yet
that the sword-hatred   between son-in-law
85 and father should waken   after fierce slaughter.

Then that sorry soul   suffered awhile,
most miserably,   he who in murk lingered.
Alone he listened   to the delight each day,
human happiness,   the hall loud with glee;
90   sweet was the singing,   sound of harping.
One learnèd in lore   made a lay singing
how the mighty King   molded creation,
fair shining fields,   far streams circling.
The proud Victor placed   pure light to brighten,
95   moonbeams and sun's rays   for mainland dwellers,
decorated   downs and meadows
with limbs and leaves.   Life, too, He gave
to each quick creature   that courses earth's paths.
Thus that group of men   gleefully lived
100   with smiles and laughter   until a single foe
began harmful works,   a hellish demon.
That ghastly grim one,   Grendel, they called him,
was that fiend of fens   who defended the waste,
marsh and moorland.   Where the monsters dwell
105   that gloom-weary ghoul   guarded a season
after the Creator   had outlawed the cursed one
among the kin of Cain.   The King of heaven
had avenged Abel   for his violent death;
in that feud he found   no favor of the Master,
110   Who banished him   from bounds of men.
Thence uncouth creatures   crept forth, both giants,
elves and ettins,   orcs, rocs followed—
those that had battled long   against blessed God,
Who sent, to right wrongs done,   retribution.
II   115   He went then seeking   soon after nightfall
for that high hallcourt,   that was inhabited
by able Danes   after ale-drinking.
Within there he noticed   a noble company,
sleeping after feasting,   sorrow unthought of,
120   care-load of mankind.   The creature of evil,
grim and greedy,   was gripped at once
by wrath and raging   and in their rest seized on
thirty thaneguards—theft and murder.
Jubilant with booty   he journeyed homeward,
125   with surfeit of slaughter   seeking his dwelling.

Men all witnessed    in the mounting light
the grim revelation,    Grendel's warwork;
then after wine and joy    weeping uprose,
moaning in the morning.    The mighty leader,
130    prince, peerless one,    depressed sat joyless.
The strong man suffered,    stricken and mournful,
when they looked at last    on the loathed foot-track
of that cursed spirit;    that combat was excessive,
long and loathsome.    No longer was it
135    than a single night    till the slayer returned,
murderous, cruel,    nor did he mourn therefore,
for felony and feuding;    he was too fixed in those.
Then was easily found    one who elsewhere slept,
in roomier quarters    resting apart,
140    closeted couches,    when it was clearly seen,
pointed out plainly,    proved to be certain,
the hate of that hallthane.    Hunted by that foeman,
surer and farther    each sheltered him after.
So he tyrannized,    turned from justice,
145    he at odds with all.    Empty was the meadhall
on that lonely hill.
                    A long interval,
time of twelve winters,    true Hrothgar, the Dane,
suffered sorrow,    besetting gloom,
every trouble.    So to all warriors
150    and to their kith and kin    was made clearly known,
gloomily by griefsong,    that Grendel battled
a season with Hrothgar.    Seething with hatred,
malice and evil,    many winters
he had waged warfare,    nor did he wish for peace
155    with any man    of the army of Danes,
nor mitigate murder    by moneys paid,
nor should thoughtful men    think it likely
to have kinder cure    at the killer's hands.
Ruthless, morose,    the ravager hunted
160    skilled troops of youths,    skulked and plotted;
that dark deathshadow    dominated
the misty moorlands.    Men know not where
hellphantoms whirl,    homeless they wander.

Thus many murders   mankind's foeman,
165 loathed lonestalker,   often allowed himself,
harsh humblings.   Hart he commanded,
the adorned meadhall   in the dark night-time.
He might never near   the noble high-seat;
he found no favor   before the Lord.
170 That was deep dolor   for the Danish king,
grief of spirit.   They gathered then
in secret counsel,   considered well
what might be best pursued   for the bravehearted,
seeking success   at sudden onslaught.
175 At times they tended   temple altars,
ordered offerings,   asking, beseeching
that the soulslayer   succor them all
against the country's curse.   Such were their customs then,
hope of heathens;   hell they remembered
180 in their heart and soul,   high God they knew not,
His law and judgment,   the Lord God unfelt;
nor did they hail Him   Heaven's Protector,
glorious Ruler.   Grief to those who shall
through dire malice   condemn the spirit
185 to the clasp of flame,   comfort not hoped for,
nor chance of changing!   Cheer to those permitted,
after their fatal day,   to find the Master,
and in the lap of the Lord   look for refuge.

III      Halfdane's successor   in heavy sorrow
190 brooded ever;   the brave man could not
stave off the strife,   the struggle was too bitter,
loathed and lasting,   that lay on his people,
fierce malignance,   fell night-evil.
Hygelac's kinsman,   high-ranked by Geats,
195 gleaned by asking   Grendel's doings.
Beowulf the brave   was best, strongest
of mighty warriors   at that moment then
of an honored life.   He ordered a vessel,
best on breakers,   said he was bound elsewhere
200 seeking the war-king   over the swan's pathway,
since the renowned ruler   had need of warriors.

Men with insight    muttered little
at that enterprise,    though they all loved him,
heartened their hero    and heeded omens.
205    The chief had chosen    choice fighting men
of those he found finest    of the foremost Geats,
bravest of men.    He brought to the seashore
fifteen fellows    to fare in that vessel;
a skilful seaman    described the coastline.
210    Time traveled on,    the transport on the seaway,
the ship under sheer cliffs,    shore swept with waves,
with winding currents.    Willingly fighters
mounted the gangway;    men carried in
to the hollow hold    handsome armor,
215    well-made war-gear.    Warriors started,
launched the vessel    on its longed-for course.
Off across the ocean,    urged by breezes,
foamy fore-stem    flew like a bird,
till by the set season    of the second day
220    the craft with curved prow    had covered the distance,
and those sailing men    saw land ahead,
shorecliffs shining,    sheer escarpments,
wide seaheadlands;    waters were traversed,
travel ended.    The troop of Weders
225    disembarked quickly,    bounded landward,
moored the wavefloater,    (mailcoats resounded,
thick protectors.)    They gave thanks to God
for a calm passage    crossing the seapaths.
Then the Scyldings' watch,    who on shore kept guard
230    along the coastal wall,    saw from the cliffsummit
bucklers on the bulwarks,    bright shields hanging,
casques and mail ready.    Questions assailed him,
tormented his mind,    who these men might be.
Hrothgar's watchman    rode to the seastrand,
235    his steed striding;    stoutly he brandished
a weighty war-spear    and, well-mannered, asked:
"Who may ye be,    having armor,
defensive corslets,    who have fared hither
over the waterways,    the windswept vessel
240    guided across ocean?    Guard of the seashore
for a time am I,    trusted watchman,

so that on Danish lands   no dreaded foemen
could inflict damage   with a fleet of ships.
Targe-bearing men   have not touched this land
245 more openly,   nor have you met, surely,
leave of warriors,   license of kinsmen.
Never have I noted   among noble men
a greater on ground   than that grand fellow,
a warrior in war-gear.   He is no waiting-man,
250 honored by his armor,   unless his aspect lies,
his peerless appearance.   Now I propose to know
your ancestry   before you enter here,
faring further   as informers hence
on the strand of Danes.   For you strangers all,
255 seavoyagers,   a simple question:
whence come you now?   I call for answer.
Recount to us clearly,   for quickest is best."

IV        The leader of men,   lord of that vessel
then replied to him   in plain discourse:
260 "We are young warriors   of the Geatish folk,
Hygelac's henchmen,   hearthcompanions.
My father was famous   in folkmoot and hall,
an able chieftain,   Ecgtheow, his name.
He passed plentiful years   ere he departed life,
265 old in earth's ways.   All wise thinkers
throughout the ample earth   easily recall him.
With friendly feelings   we have fared hither
seeking your lord,   son of Halfdane,
guard of the people.   Be our good tutor!
270 A mighty mission   to your master have we,
to the sovereign of Danes.   Not concealed should be
our notion, I think.
                    "You know if it is,
as we certainly   heard said to us,
that among the free Scyldings   some foe or other,
275 a hidden hater   'neath the helm of night
overawes enemies   with envious hate,
bloodshed, abasement.   I can to brave Hrothgar
counsel action   through a kindly heart,
how he, prudent, good,   may overpower the fiend
280 if evil outrage   ever changes

[ 28 ]

and deliverance    alleviates after,
and care, surging,    cools yet again,
or ever after    anguished suffers
distressing straits,    while there stands on high
285  the best of houses    there abiding aloft."
      Then the watch declaimed,    waiting on horseback,
fearless official:    "A far-sighted man
may sense and see,    if he consider well,
between words and works    wise distinctions.
290  Friendly forces    I find you, seeking
the Prince of Scyldings.    Depart bringing
shields and weapons;    I will show the way
and tell retainers    to tend your vessel,
that was freshly tarred,    against foes, pirates,
295  as it swings to mooring    in the sea-haven,
until the crook-necked craft    carries homeward
on coiling currents    to coasts of Geats
the well-loved warrior,    working kindness.
May God grant him    the gift most welcome,
300  that he survive wholly    ventures in battle."
      Forth they fared marching.    Fast at anchor
the broad-beamed vessel    bided, resting,
roped to the mooring.    Raised boar-figures
gleamed on cheek-plates,    golden, chiseled,
305  bright brazed with fire.    The brave spirit
sheltered shield-bearers.    Shipmen hastened
in step striding,    until there stood gables,
trimmed and timbered,    traced with gilding,
the most excellent    for earthdwellers
310  of halls under heaven    in which the high-king lived;
that light illumined    many lands around.
That brave one in battle    brought them forward
to behold the hall    of high-mettled men,
that they might find it out,    forward going.
315  Then the trail leader    turned his stallion:
"I must go from you.    God, Ruler of all,
keep you in kindness    secure on your journey!
Now I must return    to protect the shore
against fierce forces,    foes from seaward."

The path, paved with stone,   pointed direction
for clustered men.   Corslets shimmered,
hard-linked by hand,   handsome ring-mail
jingled on jerkins.   They journeyed marching
forth to the fair hall   in frightening war-gear.
325   Sea-weary men   settled their broadshields,
stout, stormhardened,   stacked at the wallside.
They bent to the benches,   breastcoverings rang,
war-gear of warriors,   weapons, javelins,
and seamen's armor   assembled together,
330   ashenshafts, gray-tipped;   the iron company
supplied with pikes.
                              Then a proud warrior
asked the fighting-men   of their family line:
"From whence bring ye   blue-gray mailcoats,
and your varnished shields,   your visored helmets,
335   a heap of hardshafts?   I am herald and thane
of stern Hrothgar.   Not a stranger has come
braver appearing   with such bounty of men.
You come for daring deeds,   not as condemned exiles,
and with greatness of heart   would greet Hrothgar."
340   For him the famous one   framed an answer,
proud prince of Geats,   he replied speaking,
hardy under helmet:   "We are Hygelac's men;
his board we share;   Beowulf, my name.
I wish Halfdane's son   to hear my errand,
345   a famous chieftain,   your friendly ruler,
if he will grant to us   that we may greet him now,
chief of the Scyldings."   Cheerfully spoke
Wulfgar of the Wendels,   wise, valorous,
and in character,   credited by many:
350   "I shall inquire at once   of the king of Danes,
to us a glad giver,   glorious ruler,
and friendly leader,   and will inform him you come
as you requested me,   recount your journey
and early tell you   how he answers you,
355   as it may seem fitting   to that fine master."
He turned then quickly   to the troop of warriors
where Hrothgar sat   ready among them.
The honored lord   was then old, graying.

Wulfgar walked forward    aware of custom,
360   famed for courage,    said to his friendly chief:
"People of Geatland    have plowed the waves
across the sweep of sea    sailing hither;
those fine fighters    call their foremost lord
Beowulf the prince.    They now beg of you
365   an exchange of words,    my chieftain Hrothgar.
Do not refuse those men    the favor of an answer,
gracious leader.    Regarded worthy
of the esteem of men,    they stand here in war-gear,
indeed their captain comes,    a competent leader,
370   showing the way hither    to those war heroes."

VI       Hrothgar answered,    ruler of Scyldings:
"I knew him first,    naught but a child:
for his late father,    loyal Ecgtheow,
received from Hrethel    his sole daughter,
375   brought home as bride.    Their brave successor
now comes seeking    kindly friendship.
Moreover seafarers    have said to us,
when they transported gifts    from people of Geatland
here in thanksgiving,    that thirty men's power
380   he had in his handgrip—    this, the hero's force
of his hard embrace.    The holy Father
guides him to us,    from His graciousness,
as I have hoped for,    that he halt Grendel's
terror in Denmark.    Treasure I should offer
385   to that dear ally    for daring courage.
Go now hastening,    herald their entrance
to see assembled    these associates.
Welcome them hither    in words of kindness
from the Danish folk."

                          [To the door hurried
390   the well-known warrior],*    gave that word within:
"The ruler of the Ring-Danes,    my righteous master,
has learned of your lineage    and he allows me to say
that you are welcome to him    from across wave-surges,
resolute seamen,    arriving in Denmark.
395   Now ye all may enter    in your armored coats
under dread helmets    to address Hrothgar.

Let the battleboards   and baneful weapons
wait the outcome   of his words' import."
Then the strongman stood   with many staunch soldiers
400   a warlike warriorband.   Some waited there,
guarded the weapons   at the good man's word.
Together they hastened   guided by the herald
under Hart's roofbeams.   [The hero entered]*
hardy under his helmet,   at the hearth he stopped.
405   Beowulf was spokesman   —his breastmail glinted,
corslet crafted   by a cunning smith—
"Hail to you Hrothgar!   I am Hygelac's kin,
his young retainer.   In youth I ventured
on many exploits.   The matter of Grendel
410   became known fully   on my native soil;
seafarers said   that this same mansion,
best of buildings,   is for the boldest Danes
empty and idle   after the evening light
comes to be covered   in the confines of sky.
415   Then my faithful friends,   finest of comrades,
instructed me strongly   to strive to find you,
my lord, Hrothgar,   for they lauded my gifts,
both my power and skill,   proved before them.
They had seen it themselves   when I sought them again,
420   bloodstained from foes,   where I bound some five,
quelled the giants,   killed in the water
seamonsters dire,   suffered affliction,
crushed the vicious   for their crimes toward Geats—
they had looked for defeat.   Now alone I come
425   to settle the conflict   against the savage foe,
Grendel, the giant.   Do grant to me,
prince of proud Danes,   as I pray of you,
chief of the Scyldings,   one choice favor.
May you not refuse me,   defender of heroes,
430   friendly folkleader,   since so far I came,
may I alone labor   and my loyal band,
this cluster of comrades,   that we may cleanse this hall.
I have also discovered   that that cruel beast,
confident, incautious,   cares for no weapon;
435   I shun to shoulder   shield against him,
or to swing a sword,   soon when I meet him.

[ 32 ]

Thus may be Hygelac   happy in spirit,
my gracious master,   that I in my grasp shall seize
the fiendish felon,   and with him fight to death,
440   loathed against loathing.   He must believe in fate,
in the day of doom,   when death takes him.
I trust his intention   —if he tries as he did—
is to feed fearless,   as so frequently
in that warchamber,   on the Weder folk.
445   Theirs was great glory.   In no grave of mine
need you hide my head,   for he hauls elsewhere,
bloodstained, bleeding   bodies of victims.
He will carry off my corpse   counting on feasting,
ruthlessly rend   in his reddened lair
450   this lonely wanderer.   No longer need you
bother for my body,   board and welfare.
If I am slain fighting,   send to Hygelac afar
my best battledress,   my breastcover,
heritage of Hrethel,   a handsome raiment,
455   work of Weland.   Wyrd guides as it must."

VII            Regal Hrothgar spoke,   ruler of Scyldings:
"For former fights,   friend of mine, Beowulf,
seeking honor   you sought us here.
The fiercest feuding   your father kindled
460   made him the slayer   of that Heatholaf
among the Wylfing clan;   then for warterror
kinsmen, the Geats,   dared not keep him near.
Thence he sought seapaths   to southern Denmark,
over the rolling waves   and reached the Scyldings.
465   Then I first controlled   folk of Denmark
and in boyhood held   all this broad country,
heroes' high castle.   Then was Heregar dead,
my elder brother,   offspring of Halfdane,
breathing no more;   he was better than I!
470   Then later I settled   that savage feud.
I sent to the Wylfings   over the waters' sweep
ancient treasure;   oaths he swore me.

     "Bitter for me telling   my breast's secret
to any person,   the awful humbling
475   heaped on Heorot   by those hateful schemes,
Grendel's grim plotting.   Now is my gallant host,

warband diminished,   wiped out by fate
into Grendel's grasp.   God surely can
frustrate the fierce deeds   of the fell mangler.
480    Often daring thanes,   drinking from flagons,
valiantly vowed   vigilant waiting
in the dark beerhall,   drunk, expecting
Grendel's coming,   with greedy blades.
Then was the meadhall   in the morning light
485    drenched with dark blood,   when day brightened
all of the bench-planking   blood-damp, darkened,
the hall gore-clotted;   and of my henchmen few,
dear, doughty ones;   death took them all.
Sit now at supper   and unseal your thoughts
490    to heroes on the hallbench   as your heart urges."
     Then was a bench prepared   in the banquet-hall
for Geatish warriors;   they yielded room.
Thither the stronghearted   strode to their places,
proud in their power.   Pourers attended
495    who bore beakers   bright ale-goblets
serving sweetened drink.   One sang at times
lilting in Hart.   There was delight for men,
no dearth of warriors,   Danish and Geatish.
VIII    Unferth spoke out,   Ecglaf's scion,
500    from below at foot   of the lord of Danes,
disclosed a covert grudge,   quarrel of rivals,
The voyage hither   vexed him deeply,
Beowulf's coming,   brave seafarer's,
for he admitted none   did more to win
505    fame on the earth   so fervently,
"Are you that Beowulf,   Breca's opponent,
rival swimmer   on the rolling sea,
where you two ventured   vainly boasting,
daring the waves   in deep waters,
510    lives at hazard?   None could lure you home,
neither friend nor foe,   or your folly undo.
     "A dangerous journey   you dared swimming;
sea-currents swirled,   swept over shoulders.

You took to ocean paths,   arms in motion,
515 swimming over seaways,   with the surging tide,
winter waves boiling.   You two in water's power
toiled for seven days;   swimming he beat you,
having more of might,   when he at the morning hour
waded from the water   on the War-Reams' coast.
520 From there he headed   home to the Brondings,
his own holding,   honored by his people—
a fortress so fair   where the folk were his,
towns and treasure.   Truly he settled
his boast besting you,   Beanstan's offspring.
525 I foresee from you   a sorry showing,
though in bold attack   or bitter fighting
you have won till now,   waiting for Grendel
nightlong—if you dare—   in the nearby gloom."
   Beowulf answered,   brave son of Ecgtheow:
530 "Well, my friend Unferth,   you have fed us much
of Breca's ventures,   beerdrunk, prating,
and what tales you tell!   Truly I assure you,
I had more power   on those murky waves,
hardships on high seas,   than any hero before.
535 We two had boasted   boyishly eager—
we were young, trusting   in our youth and strength—
that we would challenge the seas,   chancing our lives
on the vast ocean,   and that vow we kept.
We had swords at hand   as we swam outward,
540 hard, naked blades   to hack at monsters,
for we planned defense.   Not a pace could he,
nor would I from him,   ever wander
far on the floodtide   faster than the other.
Then we were together   on the gray sea afloat
545 until the flood forced us   after five nights apart,
weltering waters,   weather coldest,
dark deepening,   a dreary northwind,
war-harsh, whipped us,   waves unrelenting.
Rage roused seafish.   I was ready armed
550 to meet their malice;   my mailshirt was proof,
hard handtwisted,   helped to save me,

bright battledress   my breast covered,
with gold adorned.   In his grip the foe,
harsh hateslayer,   hauled me downwards
555   to the ground in his grasp.   But it was granted me
to pierce the creature   with my point deeply,
with the warweapon;   wild combat slew
the sinewy seabeast   through my single arm.

VIIII      "Thus frequently   fearful monsters
560   assailed me sorely.   As was suitable,
I paid them richly   with my precious sword.
They had little joy,   loathed criminals,
at their future feast,   feeding on me there,
seated at banquet   on the seabottom.
565   But in the morninglight,   maimed by weapons,
up lay they all   by the ebbtide mark,
slain by swordblows.   Since then no longer
on the high seaways   have they hindered the course
of ocean sailors.
                  "From the east came light,
570   bright beam of God;   billows lessened.
I beheld looming   high escarpments,
stormbeaten steeps.   The stars will spare
the fortune-favored   when he has fortitude!
Yet with my sword I slew   of those seamonsters
575   nine in the night-time.   I have never heard
of harder struggle   under heaven's roof,
nor a more forlorn swimmer   on the lonely seas.
Yet I survived the strain,   venture weary,
from the foes' embrace.   Then the flood bore me
580   leeward to land   on the Lappish shore,
in weltering waters.
                  "Not a word of you
in such serious straits   or such swordterror
was brought abroad.   Breca never made
equal effort   nor either of you
585   so daringly   did deeds of war
with your own two blades*—   not that I shall boast—
though you were butcher   to your brothers before,
dearest of kin;   you'll be damned in Hell
for that wicked work,   though your wit avail.

590     "I tell you as truth,   trueborn of Ecglaf,
        that never had grim Grendel,   the grisly monster,
        worked such malice   against your warlike prince,
        humbling the hall,   if your heart had been
        brave in battle   as you boast of it.
595     But he has discovered   no skilful parry
        to his fierce fighting   by your fellows here,
        nor need deeply dread   the Danish victors.
        He forced full tribute,   favored no one
        of the proud Scyldings.   Pleasure rules him;
600     he now strikes, destroys,   no strife expecting
        more than yesternight.   But the Geats and I
        shall offer combat   openly showing
        vigor and valor.   Venture who will
        boldly in this building   after break of day
605     tomorrow morning   when on mankind shines
        in the south the sun,   swathed in glory!"
          Then was the giftgiver,   grayhaired, war-famed,
        happy on the high seat.   Help he trusted,
        proud prince of Danes,   people's shepherd,
610     heard Beowulf speak   his heartfelt resolve.
          There was laughter of men,   delightful chorus;
        words were lighthearted.   Wealhtheow stepped forth
        careful of custom,   consort of Hrothgar,
        gold glittering,   greeted the hallthanes,
615     and that gracious queen   gave the first cup
        to the lord of the land,   leader of the people,
        hoped him happy   at the hall-feasting.
        Dear to Danemen,   he drank gladly:
        feast, flagon he shared,   that famous king.
620     Princess of Helmings   passed through the hall.
        In every quarter   she offered the goblet
        to tried and untried,   until the time arrived
        that the ring-decked queen,   royal in spirit,
        brought the beaker   to Beowulf the Geat.
625     She greeted the guest   then to God gave thanks
        with words of wisdom   that her wish was fulfilled,
        hope for a hero   to help in trouble,
        a protector to trust.

                              The intrepid chief
          quaffed from the goblet    that Queen Wealhtheow brought,
630    Eager for battle    he opened discourse,
          Ecgtheow's offspring,    able Beowulf:
          "When I set out to sea    I sincerely vowed
          as I sailed southward    with my circle of men
          that I by all means    would act to do
635    your people's pleasure    or perish in battle,
          fast gripped by the fiend.    Firmly I offer
          manly meetings    or in this meadhall here
          look for my life's end!"    The lady was glad,
          well pleased at words    to the wish of Danes,
640    brave words of Beowulf.    She went broidered with gold,
          courtly consort,    queen to her ruler.
                    Then again as before    great speech they made
          in the vaulted hall,    victory boasting
          of proud people,    until presently
645    the son of Halfdane    sought willingly
          his night's repose,    knowing the monster
          was ready to ravage    that royal mansion
          when the sun was seen    sinking westward,
          until darkening    dusk descended;
650    shadowy shapes    showed in the darkness
          under the cloak of clouds.    The company arose.
          Hrothgar addressed    resolute Beowulf,
          wished him well now    in his watch that night
          to win the winehall.    These words he spoke:
655    "None have I trusted    since I took up arms,
          war-gear and weapons,    to watch for me
          the Danish stronghold    until this day you came.
          Now you may have and hold    this house of splendor.
          Be mindful of glory,    show might, courage,
660    watch out for the wicked.    No wish be neglected
          if you survive in vigor    that valorous deed."
x                   Hrothgar departed    with his ring of men,
          shield of Scyldings;    they shunned the hall.
          The warleader went    to Wealhtheow his lady
665    queen and consort.    The King of glory
          had found a defender,    as fellows learned,

                                          [ 38 ]

to go against Grendel,  guarding from ogres
both place and prince  in private service.
For the chief of Geats  chose reliance
670 on the grace of God,  on grit and strength
Then he laid aside  his linked mailshirt,
the helm from his head,  gave his hammered sword,
best iron blade,  to the boy servant,
told him to watch well  the war-equipment.
675     Beowulf, the Geat,  boasted a little,
encouraged his comrades  before coming to rest:
"I count my fighting form  not inferior,
regarding exploits,  than Grendel his;
therefore slaughter by sword  I forswear, trying
680 to shed his lifeblood—  though I surely could.
Unaware of weapons  to wield against me
and to split my shield—  though his spiteful deeds
are all known widely—  he and I tonight must meet,
forsaking swordplay,  if he dare seek from me
685 war without weapon.  Afterwards the wise Ruler,
our holy Father,  on either hand may judge
fame and fortune,  as seems fitting to Him."
    The battle-brave warrior  then bowed to rest,
face found pillow,  and his followers,
690 sound seafarers,  sank to the hallbeds.
To none it seemed likely  he should leave Denmark
and behold at hand  the home he loved,
folk and freetown,  where he was formed and trained,
but they had discovered  there had escaped too few
695 from death, dire murder  of the Danish folk
in that lofty hall.  But the Lord granted
Sea-Geats success,  gave them solace, help,
fortunate fate,  so that foe of theirs
many conquered  through the might of one
700 by his own power.  Almighty God,
to tell the truth,  controlled ever
the days of man.
                In the dark night came
the shadow-prowler.  But the shipmen slept
who should be guarding  the gabled hall;

705 one only watched.   Well did men know
that unless allowed   as the Lord willed it,
that dread demon   could not drag them off,
but the one waiting   watched in anger,
filled with fury,   to see the fight's result.

XI 710   Then from the moorland   under misty hills
Grendel came gliding;   God's wrath he bore.
That murderer meant there   in the mighty hall
to seek to ensnare   some man or other.
He strode under stormclouds   till the stronghold loomed,
715 gleaming golden,   with gilded plating
disclosed clearly.   He had come before
to maraud, ravage   Hrothgar's home.
He had not found in life   before nor since
harder misfortune   than in the hall of Geats.

720   Then to the building came   the brute wandering,
deprived of pleasure.   Yet the portal gaped,
though fast with forged bands,   as he first touched it.
Angry he opened   the entrance to the building
with hateful purpose.   Hurriedly crossing
725 the patterned pavement   the oppressor came
in fuming fury.   From the fiend's eyes shot
lurid light flashing   like lightning glare.
In the hall he beheld   heroes in plenty,
a cluster of kinsmen   caught there sleeping,
730 huddled warriors.   Then his heart rejoiced;
the horrid hellfiend   hoped before daylight
to outrage each one,   all flesh riven,
breath from body.   He was blindly sure
of his fill feasting.
                              But no further prey
735 would his lot allow   when this last night passed,
no more of mankind.   The mighty chief waited,
kinsman of Hygelac,   saw how the cruel fiend
snatched suddenly   with his swift talons.
Nor did that loathed one   delay a moment;
740 when the occasion came   he clutched instantly
a sleeping warrior,   slit him greedily,
bit bone and flesh,   blood engorging,
glutted on gobbets,   gulping hands and feet.

Soon he consumed all   in his slobbering greed,
745   all that lifeless one.   Then he lurched nearer,
with his hands he grasped   toward the high-minded
captain couched there,   clutching at him,
with hellish claws.   The hero seized him,
ill intending,   and on his arm he leaned.
750   The sinful creature   saw then straightway
that he had not encountered   in any corner of earth
in its utmost realms   in other men
a harder handgrip.   In his heart he was
frightened and fearful;   flee he could not.
755   He was set to escape,   to seek a hide-out
in his devils' den.   He was not dealt with there
as in earlier days   ever he met with.
Hygelac's kinsman,   the hardy one, recalled
his evening speeches.   Up he stood then,
760   fastened upon him   till his fingers cracked.
The monster moved off;   the man stepped forward.
The creature intended,   when he could do so,
wider wheeling   to get away from there,
flee fenward thence.   He knew the fingerstrength
765   in that galling grasp.   A grievous visit
the hatekiller   made to Hart that night!
The thanehall thundered;   to the thronging Danes,
to the burghers and warriors,   to the bold it was
an end of alefeasts.*   Angered were both foes,
770   furious defenders.   The fortress resounded.
There was great wonder   that the gracious hall
withstood the strife,   the stately building
did not fall to earth;   but it was fastened well
inside and out   with iron bonding,
775   cleverly clasping.   It has come to me
that many a meadbench   with its markings of gold
was wrenched from the floor   where the wrathful fought.
Counselors of Scyldings   counted on no one
ever being able   in any way
780   to crush it by cunning,   crack it open,
beautiful, bonetrimmed,   unless the blaze's maw
swallowed it in swelter.

                                  Then a swelling scream,
        startling, arose.   Stunning terror
        numbed the North-Danes,   and the nearby churls,
785     all who heard the howl   from the high ramparts,
        God's foe grieving   in a ghastly cry
        at hopeless ruin.   Hell's captive roared,
        bewailing his wounding.   The warrior, strongest
        of men in might   in many countries
790     while life lingered,   had locked him fast.
XII     The warriors' protector   wished not at all
        to release alive   that life-destroyer,
        nor count useful   to country or people
        one breath of his lifetime.
                                  Thereupon Beowulf's men
795     most eagerly drew   heirlooms of steel
        for the life of their lord;   their illustrious prince
        they meant to cover   when they might do so.
        They did not reckon   on reaching the struggle,
        those brave-minded   battle-fighters,
800     aiming to assail him   from every side
        seeking his soul:   no sword of war,
        not any on earth   of iron most splendid,
        could mar or touch   that miscreant.
        For he had bewitched by spells   weapons of conquest,
805     every edged weapon.   The end of his lifespan
        was to be in misery   in those diminishing days
        of his earthly course   and that alien
        must travel far   controlled by fiends.
        Then he who often before   with evil relish
810     had wrought ravage   toward the race of man—
        he was foe to God—   found that his body
        would not serve him more,   but the sister's child,
        Hygelac's nephew,   high in spirit,
        had his arm gripped fast;   each while he lived
815     hated the other.   Hot pain anguished
        the shape of terror;   on his shoulder spread
        a great gash bursting,   gaping sinews,
        breaking the bone-case.   Beowulf was granted
        glory in battle;   and thence Grendel fled,

                            [ 42 ]

820 fatally wounded,   under fen-clad hills
to his unhappy home.   Here readily
he realized fully   his reckoning ceased,
his days were numbered.

                                        Danes had their wish
after bloody battle   best hopes fulfilled.
825 One had fared from afar   to free the people;
he saved Hrothgar's hall   from rude assault.
Stout-hearted, astute,   in strife he gloried,
and that night-combat.   To the Northern Danes
the captain of Sea-Geats   had kept his promise;
830 rough ravages   he also remedied.
Sorrow from evil   suffered earlier,
and driven by force   they endured often
no small affliction.   That was a signal proof
when the mighty man   mounted the hand
835 arm and shoulder—   there altogether
was Grendel's grip—   under the gabled roof.
XIII       Then in the morning,   as men tell us,
about that mighty hall   many a warrior
fared with their chieftains   from far and near,
840 on wide ways thronging   to witness that marvel,
his fearsome footprints.   Nor did his fated end
dismay a man   minded to look on
track and trailpath   of the troll disgraced,
how he went his way   weary-hearted,
845 conquered in combat   to the kelpies' pool,
doomed and driven   dripping a blood-spoor.
There on the brimming brink   the bloody waters,
fearful flux of waves   fought and mingled;
blood surged boiling,   bright drops from swords;
850 doomed to death, hiding,   withdrawn from pleasure,
he lay down his life then   in his lair amid fens,
his heathen heart there;   Hell received him.
      Thence all returned,   old companions:
a joyous journey   joined by young men
855 proudly prancing   on powerful horses
from the troubled pool.   They talked together
of Beowulf's exploit,   and boasted often

that in north or south   none surpassed him
from sea to sea   below the sweep of sky,
860   on the broad earth best   who bore weapons,
worthiest of a kingdom.   Yet with their warrior prince
they found no fault,   a friendly leader,
gracious Hrothgar,   for he was a goodly king.
At times the battle-brave   in bouts of racing
865   urged their sorrel steeds   swiftly running
on country byways   that they counted smoother,
choicest they knew.   At times a chosen thane,
a vaunted speaker,   versed in measures,
he who remembered much,   many a story,
870   tales of the ancients,   told them in style,
faithfully fashioned.   Foremost he mentioned,
cleverly recounted   the coming of Beowulf.
He spoke with talent,   spinning the tale,
wove words in verse.   Well he recounted
875   Sigemund's valor,   what was said to him
of high deeds of courage,   of hidden secrets,
the Wælsing's combats   and the wide journeys
of which sons of men   seldom had heard,
feuds and offenses,   except Fitela there,
880   when he told of talk,   tales related,
uncle to nephew   always together,
comrades in need   in all conflicts met.
Many a giant   of the monsters' race
sank from sword-blows.   Sigemund's glory—
885   fame follows death—   flourished spreading:
dragon-slayer   daring in battle,
hoard keeper's bane;   the high-born fighter
dared death alone,   dangerous venture,
nor was Fitela near   at the frost-gray cave.
890   Good luck granted   that his glaive struck home
through that speckled snake.   His splendid weapon
stuck in the stonewall.   Strife quelled the wyrm.
Thus the war-victor   won by his courage
right without contest   to the ring-treasure,
895   what wealth he chose   the Wælsing might claim,
bearing bright armor   to the broad vessel,
deeply laden.   The dragon had melted.

[ 44 ]

He was of banished men    best known the widest
among tribes of men,    protector of warriors;
900    by mighty exploits   he had met success
after Heremod's heart,    high deeds and power
weakened, waning.    Forthwith murdered
when betrayed to Jutes    and tribal justice,
Heremod, too long    hampered by troubles,
905    became to high and low    a heavy burden
and a great grievance.    Goodly thinkers,
looking to him    for relief from ills
in former seasons,    fretted at his conduct,
his daily deeds    a disappointment.
910    The prince, they thought,    would prosper and thrive,
taking his father's rank,    defending his people,
riches and stronghold,    the realm of heroes,
home of the Scyldings.    Hygelac's nephew
became a fairer friend    to his fellow men;
915    crime claimed the first,    cruel Heremod.
          At times contending    along tawny roads
steeds strove to win.    Stars fled, day waked,
swept on swiftly.    Many a soldier came,
high-hearted men,    to that hall dwelling
920    for that curious sight,    likewise the king, himself,
guardian of treasure;    glorious he entered
from his chamber apart    with chosen escort,
culled of the keenest,    and his queen besides
walked toward the winehall    with her women's troop.

XIIII

925          Hrothgar spoke out,    he reached the hall,
stood on the steps,    saw the steep gable
gleaming golden    and Grendel's arm.
"To the Almighty    let us offer thanks
for the sight granted!    I have suffered much
930    grief and grim anguish    from Grendel's malice.
Wonder after wonder    is the work of God.
Not so long ago    I had looked in vain
and found no aid ever    for all those troubles,
no hope of healing,    when the hall, superb,
935    battle-bloodied    stood bathed in gore.
There was widespread woe    for wise counsellors
hardly hoping    ever to hold secure

[ 45 ]

the fine folk-stronghold    against fiends, devils,
and determined intruders.    A trusted soldier
940    through God's power    has gained success
that we formerly failed    to force by cunning.
What bride soever    bore that young man,
a model of manhood,    if she remains living
may justly claim    that the Judge of all
945    cherished and blessed her    in that childbearing.
Now my Beowulf, friend,    best of warriors,
I will hold you henceforth    in my heart as son;
keep you likewise    this kinship offered.
In this new friendship    nothing will fail you
950    of worldly wishes    that my word may grant.
Often to meaner men    I meted out payment,
loaded with treasure    for less account
to those who were weaker in war.    Well have you done here
in gallant actions,    so that your glory lives
955    forever and ever.    May the Almighty
grant you good things    as He has given before!"
    Beowulf addressed him    born son of Ecgtheow:
"We have fought that fight    favored greatly,
a deed of daring,    dangerous adventure
960    against forces unknown.    Fain would I rather
you might see the foe,    himself laid low,
fiend in his apparel    fallen, despairing!
I hoped to bind him    in hard fetters
clutched quick by hand,    caught on his deathbed,
965    death agony    darkening over,
unless his body escape.    Bind him I could not,
nor his going hinder    when God was unwilling;
not hard enough I held him,    that hated foe,
deadly enemy.    He was too dire, too strong,
970    that fiend in fleeing.    Yet to effect escape
he left his hand behind,    huge paw and shoulder.
The cursed creature,    comfort denied,
will not long survive.    The loathsome killer,
crushed under sins,    cruel pain sears him,
975    fiercely enfolded    in its fearful grip
by its baleful bonds.    There must that beastly slave,
dark-stained with crimes    endure forever

until the day of doom    when his dismal fate
must follow his course    as the Father decrees."
980    Then he sat silent,    the son of Ecglaf,
without boasting speech    of battle prowess,
after the champions,    by a chieftain's might
looked on the forepaw    across the lofty vault,
on the fiend's fingers.    At the front of each
985    stiff strong talons,    like steel skewers,
ugly and awesome,    armed the great hand
of the godless fiend.    Gravely men reckoned
that no proven steel    of powerful warriors
could stab the stranger,    nor yet strike from him
990    his bloody battle-arm,    as had the brave hero.
xv    Quickly was decreed    careful handwork
on Hart Hall within;    that high building,
winehall and guest-house    workers adorned,
both men and women.    Mounted hangings,
995    gleaming golden,    graced the meadhall,
marvels to men    who had met there to gaze.
That bright building    had been badly rent
and the hinges sprung,    though held inside
by wrought-iron clasps;    only the roof remained
1000    all undamaged,    when the ugly beast,
vicious, violent,    veered off in flight,
anguished, despairing.    By no means easily
can one evade his end,    venture who wishes,
but he must reach the spot    readied beforehand
1005    for sons of men,    souls yet living,
who wander the world,    their way need-driven,
where his corpse must lie    secure forever,
sleeping after feasting.    Then at a certain hour
the son of Halfdane    sought the meadhall
1010    to share the banquet    with his shield-warriors.
I heard of no company    counted greater,
better in bearing    banded with their leader.
They seated themselves,    their success well known,
and feasted gladly.    In that famous hall
1015    Hrothgar and Hrothulf,    resolute leaders
and close kinsmen,    took cups of mead
most graciously.    The great hall within

was filled with friends.    Then no false dealings
troubled the people    of the tribe of Danes.
1020 Beowulf received    the brand of Halfdane,
a battle standard,    broidered in gold,
warhelm and buckler,    rewards for triumph,
a crowd had witnessed    the costly weapon
borne before the warrior.    Beowulf accepted
1025 the goblet in the great hall.    Those gifts caused him
no embarrassment    before the bowmen there.
I heard of no friendlier    favors offered,
gold-girt treasures,    like those gifts all four,
others were granted    among alebenches.
1030 At the helmet's crown    a head-protector
wound with wire, twisted,    warded off swordblows,
that the forged weapon,    firm in combat,
might not wound deeply,    when the warrior, armed,
must go to engage    grim opponents.
1035 Then the men's defense    commanded horses.
Four pair entered    on the floor of the hall
with burnished bridles.    One bore a saddle
artfully adorned,    honored with rich gems;
that was the high seat    when Halfdane's son
1040 sought with his soldiers    sword-play in battle.
The lordly leader    lacked no courage
when the dying dropped    down around him.
Then the steadfast king    gave him steeds and gear,
both those treasures,    to Beowulf the fearless,
1045 bade him wield them well    and wished him joy.
Thus the high ruler,    hoard protector,
rewarded warfare    with wealth and horses.
He who will tell truly,    trusting justice,
can find no fault    with such fair treatment.
XVI
1050 Besides to each sailor    on the sea-voyage,
Beowulf's companions,    the bold Scylding
gave heirlooms also    and ample treasure,
there on the alebenches,    and he offered then
to give gold in pay    for him whom Grendel slew,
1055 criminally    as he would have killed others,
unless mighty God    and that man's courage
had defended them    against that fate at last.

God governed all,   as he yet guides mankind.
Therefore remember,   keep in mind ever,
1060  forethought is best.   One will find here much
of both weal and woe   in his world journey,
long lingering   in life's conflicts.
        Melody and music   mingled together
when before Halfdane's heir   the harper recited
1065  to murmuring strings   many a story,
and then Hrothgar's bard   raised excitement
along the meadbenches   as he made a song
how the hero Hnaef,   Halfdane leader,
was to fall stricken   in a Friesian hall,
1070  when the swift onslaught   sought out the people.
        Indeed Hildeburh   need hardly praise
faith of the Jutemen.   Faultless was she,
yet lost her loved ones   in lethal conflict;
son and brother,   sorely wounded,
1075  fell doomed by spears:   feelings were a torment.
Not at all causelessly   she decried that fate,
when she, daughter of Hoc,   in the dawning light
as heaven brightened   could behold in death
her murdered kinsmen,   where she had most enjoyed
1080  all the delights of life.
                        Now were left only
a few followers   under Finn's command.
By no quick conquest   could he quell Hengest,
the prince's warrior,   on that parley floor,
nor yet dislodge the lave   left from the carnage.
1085  They sought to settle,   setting fair terms:
all cleared for them   other quarters,
hall and highseat,   that they might hold jointly,
control together   with the tribe of Jutes
and with gifts of goods   on given feastdays.
1090  Folcwalda's son   freely honored
Hengest's henchmen   with handsome rings
and as much money,   massed wealth in store,
splendid goldplate   as would spur Friesians,
his own tribe, in the alehall   to exploits of war.
1095     Then they bound in trust   on both parties
by firm friendship bonds   Finn to Hengest,

asking for oaths   (the only solution)
that he look with esteem   on the unlucky men
by all-wise counsel,   so that everyone
1100   by no word or deed   waken trouble,
nor with ill intent   ever mention
that with their leader lost   their lord's slayer
(they were forced by fate)   they followed after.
If then some Friesian   by unfriendly speech
1105   should remind the men   of mortal hatred,
a swordblade must settle   the sudden outbreak.
An oath was exacted   and ancient gold
brought from burial.   Then the best warrior,
prince of Scyldings,   was prepared for the flames.
1110   By that pyre, readied,   was plainly seen
the blood-stained breastcoat,   boar all gilded,
on hardened helmet,   highborn warriors
fallen full of wounds,   some on the field cut down.
Then did Hildeburh   bid hoist her son
1115   on her brother's pyre   to burn together,
fast in the flames,   Finn's son and hers,
by his uncle's arm.   Uttering a grief-song,
the lady lamented.   They lifted the warrior.
Smoke of slain heroes   swirled toward the sky
1120   in a roar of flames.   Raw wounds opened,
brains boiled from skulls,   blood flowed, gushing
from bursting bodies.   Burning fury
in its greed engorged   those engulfed by war
of either people,   all their glory spent.

XVII
1125   Then those soldiers left   to see again Friesland;
friends fall'n, they sought   families waiting,
homes and stronghold.   Hengest then still
through the wild winter,   wanting free choice,
lived on Finn's terms.   He longed for his homeland,
1130   but could not sail to sea   in the swift vessel,
curve-necked swimmer.   Currents weltered,
wind-blown, stormy.   Waves were ice-locked,
wintry fetters,   until there woke again
spring in farmlands,   such as spreads anew
1135   when the seasons' course   signifies duly
wondrous weather.

Then was winter past,
fair fields outspread.   Finn's guest, longing
to leave the stronghold,   yet looked to vengeance
for the wrongs suffered,   rather than sailing,
1140   if he could bring about   a bitter meeting,
where he could wreak his wrath   on the rival Jutes.
      Thus he carried out   his common duty
when he held the sword   that Hunlafing
laid on his lap there,   a lustrous blade;
1145   its keen cutting edge   had been encountered by Jutes.
      The fierce-hearted Finn   in his family home
met a dire death-blow   from a Danish sword,
when Guthlaf and Oslaf   told of grim onslaught,
and subsequent sorrow   after the sea-voyage;
1150   distressed, reproachful,   unrestrained in mood.
Then hot blood ran   and the hall reddened,
foes fell dying—   thus was Finn cut down
mid the king's own corps,   and his queen taken.
Then the brave Scyldings   bore to their vessel
1155   chattels of the household   from the chieftain's stead,
jewels likewise   and gems well wrought,
what they found of Finn's.   A fair breeze blowing,
they sailed safely   to the sea-coast of home
with that courtly queen.
                              Quiet now the singer;
1160   the tale was told.   Talk rose again,
   clamor continued;   cupbearers poured
wine from wide flagons.   Then Wealhtheow arose
going in golden crown   where that goodly couple,
nephew and father's brother,   sat together, now still at peace;
1165   each to the other was true.   Likewise Unferth the spokesman
sat close by the King of Danes;   both knew his courage was good,
that he was to his lord loyal,   though he should lack mercy
in quarrels at kinsmen's defiance.
                              Then said the queen of
                              Scyldings:
"I give this goblet,   good my master,
1170   generous giver!   Be you in joy ever,
your followers' friend.   Favor these Weders
with words of kindness;   that were well to do.

[ 51 ]

Be you gracious to Geats,   gifts remembered,
from near and far   that you now possess.
1175   There was a word told me   that you wished as son
that hero yonder.   Heorot, bright palace,
has been cleansed, made safe.   Keep while you may
the rewards of the world,   will them to kinsmen,
both people and kingdom,   when you pass away,
1180   and must face your fate.   Friendly Hrothulf
I know will keep kindly   his cousins, our children,
if you should leave the world,   lord of Scyldings,
sooner than he does.   It seems he will give them,
those sons of ours,   suitable favors,
1185   recalling kindness,   clear benefits,
offered as pleasures,   and as honors, too,
when as a little lad   he lived among us."
      Then she turned to the bench   with the two brothers,
Hrethric and Hrothmund,   Hrothgar's children,
1190   and the brave hero,   Beowulf the good,
young men together,   Geat and Scylding.
XVIII      Then a cup was brought   with courteous greeting,
offered the guest.   Armbands were shown him
made of twisted gold,   two ornaments,
1195   garments, engraved rings,   and a great collar,
best in beauty   that the broad earth holds.
None handsomer   beneath the heaven's vault
in hoarded treasure   after Hama removed
to that brilliant burg   the Brosing necklace,
1200   bright brooch and cup,   breaking from the malice
of Eormenric   he chose endless reward.
Grandson of Swerting,   goodly Hygelac,
had that linked circlet   on his last voyage,
after he braved attack   below the bannered staff
1205   defending the booty.   Fate took him off,
feuding with the Friesians;   from foolhardiness
he asked for trouble.   Ornaments he carried,
costly jewels,   over the cauldron of waves,
but the powerful prince   perished in his armor.
1210   Then the corpse of the king   was claimed by Franks,
trappings, breastmail,   and that torque besides.

Then the worst warriors    after war's carnage
plundered the bodies;    people from Geatland
could yet hold the field.
                                        The hall resounded.
1215 Wealhtheow stood forth,    spoke to the warrior troop:
"Wear this torque with joy,    a treasure of the people,
and this breast armor,    Beowulf, dear friend,
may you prosper well,    profit in fortune;
let your strength be known,    but to these stripling lads,
1220 be kind in counsel.    I shall requite you well.
You have fared in life    so that far and near,
forever and ever,    you will be honored by men
as the sea circles,    surging on rocks
or windswept escarpments.    May you well flourish,
1225 lord, while living!    With this load of wealth
may you receive all good.    To these sons of mine
be kind in conduct,    keeper of gladness!
Here is everyone    to the other true,
to his lord loyal,    lenient of spirit,
1230 nobles united,    the nation alerted;
wine-flushed warriors,    as I will, they obey."
    Then she found her seat.    The feast was splendid,
fine wine poured freely.    Fate cast no shadow,
although many a man    was marked to suffer
1235 after night should fall.    And from the noble house
Hrothgar departed    to rest in his quarters.
Countless warriors    carefully guarded
the oaken alehall,    as they often had.
They bore off benches;    bedding was spread,
1240 bolsters and pillows.    One in the banquet-hall,
foredoomed to fall,    found his hallrest.
Then at their heads they placed    the hardy bucklers,
bright body-shields.    There on the benches stood
battle-tall helmets,    breastmail shining,
1245 clearly distinguished    above courtly thanes
and strong, straight spear-shafts.    They stayed ready,
as custom decreed,    for combat always,
in the field or at home,    whenever fate summoned,
as their lord had need.    Loyal and trusting
1250 all stood ready.    That was a staunch people.

[ 53 ]

# A Grieving Mother's Vengeance:
## MONSTER-MOTHER OF THE MERE

XVIIII    Then they sank to sleep.  One sorely purchased
his evening slumber   as so often before
when Grendel guarded   the goldhall nightly,
wrongful owner,   until he reached his end
1255    at his death for his deeds.   Then it would dawn on men
that an avenger survived,   a vicious destroyer,
after the foe perished   in the fierce attack.
    Grendel's mother,   a ghastly creature,
she who must remain   remembering troubles
1260    in the dire waters   of dreaded torrents,
after Cain became   the cruel slayer
of his own brother,   offspring of his father.
The exiled outcast   occupied the wasteland;
marked by his murders,   he fled men's delight,
1265    a solitary exile.   His descendants
predestined demons,   dread Grendel, too,
a hateful haunter   who at Hart had found
a watchful warrior   awaiting combat.
The creature caught him,   clutching his arm,
1270    but he remembered well   his mighty power,
a great gift treasured,   that God had bestowed,
and he hoped for help   from that high Ruler,
solace and succor.   Thus he succeeded, downed
that fiend infernal.   Then the foe of man
1275    deprived of pleasure,   departed, humbled,
sought his deathplace.   It was a sad journey
that his mother now   meant to venture,
as greedy and gloomy   she grasped at vengeance.
Then to Hart she came   where on hall pallets
1280    slept the South Danes.   Soon those warriors
had altered fortunes,   when she entered there,
Grendel's mother.   They gauged the horror
diminished as much   as the might of women,

warcraft of females,   lacks of weaponed men's
1285   when with beaten blades   from blacksmith's forge,
swords smeared with blood,   swine ornaments
were sheared from helms   by sharpened edges.
  Then were stout swords drawn   on the stronghold's floor,
blades above benches,   broad shields in plenty
1290   held fast by hand,   helmets forgotten
and the wide corslets   as wild fear seized them.
When she was discovered,   escape her intention,
she was in haste hoping   yet to hold to life.
Clutching quickly,   she clasped a warrior
1295   as she fled fenward,   one firmly carried.
He was the dearest Dane   to dauntless Hrothgar
in his fellowship   and a fine warrior,
slaughtered sleeping,   a soldier of fame
from sea to sea.   Assigned beforehand,
1300   Beowulf was elsewhere   in better quarters,
after the treasure-gifts   to the trusted Geat.
Hart was in uproar;   but the hand she knew,
clotted, blood-stained;   she carried it with her.
Grief gripped the hall.   That was no good exchange,
1305   when both must barter   for bitter purchase
lives of loved ones.   Then was the lord, the wise
gray guardian,   grim of spirit,
when he knew that dead   lay his noble thane,
that loved warrior   lifeless, missing.
1310   At once was Beowulf fetched,   blessed with triumph.
The princely warrior   and his companions in arms
entered at daybreak   all together
where the wise one mused   waiting to discover
whether after sad tidings   the Sovereign Power
1315   ever would alter   his evil fortune.
The well-known warrior   with his worthy troop
hastened toward the highseat—   the hall-floor echoed—
to greet the great one   with gracious words,
asking the noble Dane   if night had brought him
1320   the pleasant slumber   his people wished for.

[ 56 ]

XX      Hrothgar answered,    royal Scylding:
        "Ask not of gladness!    Grief is renewed
        for the Danish folk.    Dead is Ashhere,
        elder brother    of Yrmenlaf.
1325    He was my confidant    and my counselor;
        as my close comrade    when in combat fierce
        we protected our heads    while troops clashed on foot,
        smiting boarcrests.    So should a soldier be,
        excellent always.    Such was Ashhere!
1330    Here in Heorot    a horrid spirit
        has dealt him death.    Where that dire glutton
        dragged home his corpse    to indulge her greed
        is known to me.    She brought night vengeance
        for your grievous grip    that brought Grendel's end,
1335    clasped close last night,    killed in battle,
        since he too long lessened    by liegemen's numbers,
        night after night.    Now comes another,
        a mighty murderess,    who means reprisal
        for her slaughtered son.    She seeks far afield
1340    return of outrage,    so retainers think,
        grieving for a chieftain    who gave generously,
        a bitter burden    of the breast's anguish,
        now that that hand lies still    that heeded your wishes,
        furnished you all    with favors in plenty.
1345    I heard countryfolk,    counselors too,
        my own people    earlier mention
        having seen sometimes    such a couple,
        wild wanderers,    wasteland creatures,
        wardens of moorlands.    Of them one, they say,
1350    as they most certainly    saw and told us,
        was like a woman;    the other losel wretch
        had a man's image,    though monstrous huge,
        trod the track of care,    a troll of the fenlands.
        From olden days    have the earth-dwellers
1355    named him Grendel.    They knew of no father
        nor if any might be    earlier begotten,
        unholy spirits.    They haunt a land
        of wild wolfslopes,    wind-scourged headlands,
        fearsome fentracks.    There a foaming stream

1360 down drops away   past darkening cliffs—
the flood flows beneath.   Yet not far away
by the mile-measure   the mere stretches.
Hoarfrosted heights   hang above it,
shrubs fast rooted   shade the water.

1365 In the dusk glimmers   a devilish marvel:
flame on the flood.   No freeman living,
although old and wise,   knows the unplumbed depths.
When harried by hounds,   the hart on the moorland,
the strong-horned stag at bay,   startled would seek for

1370 the frosty forest   when facing death;
give up life on the ledge   before leaping in
to hide his head   in that horrid pool.
Tumult of waters   towers spuming
to the scowling sky;   scud, blown by winds,

1375 darkens the daylight,   until dismal the gloom,
the heavens weeping.   Again our hope is in you,
you alone can help us.   The lair you know not,
it is a fearful place.   You will find waiting
that sinful soul.   Seek if you dare!

1380 I shall reward you well   with wealth for battle,
ancient treasure,   as I offered before,
twisted goldbands,   if you return safely."

XXI      Beowulf answered,   born to Ecgtheow:
"Bear bitterness!   Better for each one

1385 to avenge comrades   than in vain to grieve.
So let each of us   to the end endure
in the world's troubles.   Win glory who may
ere the day of death;   for the dead hero
that will ever be best   when the end has come.

1390 Arise, royal prince,   let us reach at once
the ground imprinted   by Grendel's avenger.
I give you my promise   she shall not depart safely,
nor in the heart of the hills,   nor the high forest,
nor the floor of the flood,   flee where she wishes!

1395 On this day may you   endure with patience
troubles whatever,   as I trust you will."
Then up sprang the ancient,   uttering his thanks
to his mighty God   for what that man had said.

Then was Hrothgar's steed    readied, bridled,
1400    a curly-maned courser.    The clear-sighted prince
rode off resplendent,    rough soldiers marched,
shield on shoulder.    The shallow traces
they followed forward    along forest paths,
a way through the woodlands    as she went forward
1405    across the murky moor    with the murdered thane,
butchered, the best    of the burg-watchers,
those who kept the court    with King Hrothgar.
Then the prince's son    passed by the cliffside,
steep and stony,    a constricted path,
1410    slim single track,    secret, unfamiliar,
craggy cliff-faces,    caves of monsters.
Forth he led them    with a few leaders,
searching the country,    seeking the fenpath,
until suddenly    he saw the cliff-trees
1415    sloping above:    the slate-gray boulder,
the woeful woodlands.    Water lay below
bloody and turbid.    Brave men of Denmark,
faithful followers,    friends of Scyldings,
must bear further    bitter heartache,
1420    anguish for each one    when Ashhere's head
was found lying    on the fell above.
    Flood surged with blood    where the folk looked down
on that horrid gore.    A horn blared at times
a fervent fighting song.    The footsoldiers paused,
1425    watching in the water    wondrous dragons,
sea-serpents writhing    sounded the ocean,
and on coastal crags,    krakens basking,
and many a monster    which as morning woke
wandered away    on watery currents
1430    and dangerous journeys.    They dropped below,
heartless, hateful,    hearing on a sudden
the blaring battlehorn.    With bow and arrow
the prince from Geatland    soon deprived of life
one sea-swimmer.    The slim hard war-shaft
1435    struck its stomach;    it stirred more slowly,
swimming to sea    as it sank in death.

Then with barbed boarspears   it was boldly attacked,
and as it dived downward,   was subdued fiercely
and hauled on the headland   from the heaving waves,
1440   a wondrous wave-roamer.   Warriors studied
the dreadful stranger.

                              Having dressed himself
in battle-armor,   Beowulf trusted
that the wide war-mail,   well-linked by hand,
would defend his life.   He had no fear at all
1445   as he explored the pool   that it would prove faulty,
or that a hostile hand   in hateful fury
should harm or hurt   his heart and vitals.
But his gleaming helm   guarded him safely;
it must seek below   through surging waters
1450   of the murky mere   his mighty helmet
worked by weapon-smith   and wondrously fashioned,
circled by a chain-guard   set with jewels,
embellished at the border   with boar figures;
no brand or battlesword   could bite through it.
1455      That was help indeed,   the hilted swordblade,
Unferth's weapon,   offered in loan
by Hrothgar's spokesman,   Hrunting its name.
That was an ancient sword,   an heirloom treasured;
its edge was iron,   etched with poison,
1460   hardened in heart's blood.   Of those who held it none
found it failing,   though in fierce battle,
nor did he who dared enter   on dangerous ventures
on fields of foemen.   That was not the first trial,
when it was to deal in deeds   of daring action.
1465      Indeed, then Ecglaf's son,   Unferth the strong,
no more remembered   his remarks before
when loud-voiced, drunken,   as he lent that sword
to a finer fighter.   He refused himself
to dare deep waters   and deeds of valor,
1470   risking his life;   there he reaped no fame,
nor honor for courage.   Not so the other man
after girding to fight   in the grim waters.
XXII      Beowulf spoke bravely,   bold Ecgtheow's son:
"Now bethink you, high one,   Halfdane's kinsman,
1475   and most prudent prince,   now impatient to go,

I repeat my speech,   patron most liberal,
if I must lose my life   in delivering you
in your need, and now   know that though lifeless,
I have fixed your place   in my father's stead.
1480 Be you guard and guide   for my gallant men,
these brave comrades,   if battle takes me.
Also the gifts of gold   you have given me,
beloved Hrothgar,   deliver to Hygelac.
Then may the chief of Geats,   child of Hrethel,
1485 gazing on the gift-heap,   that golden treasure,
know I found a friend   free in his bounty,
a generous leader,   while I might enjoy it all.
And let Unferth have   the ancient treasure,
this wondrous weapon   with well-tempered blade;
1490 I will win glory   wielding Hrunting
or I shall die today   in desperate battle.
     When these words were said   the Weders' chieftain
advanced valiantly—   advice or answer
he would not wait for;   the wild flood received
1495 the daring hero.   Much of the day had passed
before he glimpsed the ground,   the gravel bottom.
     She who had defended the flood   for fifty years,
greedy for battle,   grim and angry,
sensed already   that a certain one
1500 hunted downward   toward haunted realm.
She groped toward him,   grasped the warrior
with her cruel claws   but might not cleave open
such a sound body,   circled and protected
by buckled breastmail.   She could not break apart
1505 the hard-linked hauberk   with hostile fingers.
Then the ogress bore   the armored leader
to her deep dwelling   as she dived below.
He could not force a fight,   though firmly resisting,
nor wield his weapons;   yet water creatures
1510 assailed him swimming;   sea-beasts attacked
with savage tusks   and slit his armor;
fiends followed him.   Then he found he stood
in a hostile hall,   unharmed by water,
and the vaulted roof   prevented flooding
1515 and sudden swells   from swirling about him.

[ 61 ]

He saw fire flaming   on the floor beyond,
brilliantly burning,   a bright radiance.
   Then that worthy man   saw the witch near him,
a monstrous merewife.   He gave a mighty stroke
1520 with the battlebrand;   the blow was not weakened.
The ring-sword rang out   on her wretched head
with a wild warcry.   Then the warrior found
that the flashing sword   failed to wound her,
or injure fatally,   but the edge played false
1525 for the prince at need.   In previous conflicts,
hand-to-hand meetings,   it had hacked armor,
helmets of the doomed.   Now the handsome blade
first had faltered,   its fame diminished.
   Hygelac's nephew   hardy, resolute,
swift to action,   sought for glory.
1530 The furious fighter   flung down the blade,
richly embellished,   to rest on the ground,
strong and steel-edged.   He stoutly trusted
his mighty handgrip;   so should a man behave
1535 when in war he would   win long glory,
little troubling   for his life and fate.
   He grasped the shoulder   of Grendel's mother;
the War-Geats' leader   worried none for struggle.
Battle-hardened,   bursting with anger,
1540 he forced toward the floor   his foe, that deadly one.
She requited him well:   quickly rushing
with her grievous grip   she grasped the fighter.
The hero, disheartened,   though hardiest on foot,
stumbled, falling,   striking the ground.
1545    She sat down on the guest,   drew out her sheath-knife,
broad, burnished edge,   let the blade avenge
her only offspring.   All Beowulf's chest
bore the breast-links,   a bulwark to survival
against barb and blade   that balked wounding.
1550 The heir of Ecgtheow   would have ended his life
below the ample earth,   but armored corslet,
hard-linked hauberk,   helped the chieftain,
and the blessed Lord   brought victory.

The high King of heaven, holy Ruler,
1555 set out to save him, deciding justly
after the good leader gained his footing.
XXIII       Then he saw a sword, a siege-proved falchion
of ancient ettins with edges tempered,
a guardsman's glory. Though a greater sword
1560 than any other could ably bear,
it was the best of blades for battleplay,
featly fashioned, forged by giants.
The champion of Scyldings drew the chain-held sword
furiously and fiercely, freeing it for action.
1565 Of life despairing, he launched a blow
catching her neck with a cruel stroke,
so the bonejoints broke, the blade passed quite through
the fore-doomed body, and she fell dying;
the blade was bloody; the brave one rejoiced.
1570       Then a beam brightened, burning inside,
even as above the earth brilliantly shines
heaven's candle. Along the hall he gazed,
holding high the sword, Hygelac's retainer,
angry, resolute, edged along the cavewall.
1575 The weapon was not worthless for the warfighter,
for he sought to return swift requital
for frequent forays by the foe, Grendel,
of those done daily to Danes at Heorot,
much more often than merely once,
1580 when he slew in sleep and then swiftly devoured
retainers of Hrothgar, trusted companions,
fifteen a night of the fighting men;
others also, odious booty,
he had borne away. The bitter hero
1585 settled the score when he saw Grendel
lying lifeless on his lonely couch,
weary of warfare since wounded before
struggling in Heorot. Struck after death,
the corpse sprang open at the cut sustained,
1590 a savage swordblow that severed his head.
      At once those wisemen watching the surface
with Hrothgar beheld the raging waters,
blended, bloodstained, boiling below them.

The gray-haired old men   together related
1595  the hero's exploits,   though they could hope no more
for the prince's return,   proud, triumphant,
seeking their king,   the celebrated leader,
but the waterwolf   with wicked purpose
had laid him low,   the likeliest prospect.
1600 When the ninth hour neared,   the noble Scyldings
hastened homeward,   the height deserted;
the gold-giver, too,   gave up waiting.
The strangers stayed there,   staring at the water,
heart-sick, hoping,   hardly expecting,
1605 to see returning   himself, their lord.
    Then blood-blackened   all that blade began
wasting away;   that was wonderful,
that it all melted,   like icicles melting
when the Father frees   from frosty bindings
1610 winter waters;   He wields His power
over times and tides;   that is the true Ruler.
Though he saw much that lay   in the mere's cavern,
the trusted leader   left the treasure behind,
but for the head and hilt,   handsome with gems—
1615 the wave-traced weapon   had wasted, melted,
the blade burned outright,   that blood too scalding.
The poison-filled intruder   perished within.
He who had stood in strife   among stricken foes,
set to swimming   swiftly upward.
1620 The swirling waters   were all safely cleansed,
the roomy reaches   where the ranging troll
abandoned this brief world   and the bonds of life.
Then swimming stoutly   the seamen's protector
came at last to land;   he laughed gladly
1625 at the mighty load,   the mere's spoils he brought.
Then the thanes met him,   gave their thanks to God,
a group glorified,   gladdened by their chieftain
since they might see him safe,   sound among them.
Helm and hauberk   were hastily unbuckled
1630 from their keen captain.   Under clouds the mere,
stained by the struggle,   grew still and drowsed.

They fared forth from there   by the footpath back,
hearts high, joyous,   on the homeward road
pacing the path.   Proud followers
1635 bore the heavy load   from the heights above;
that was a toilsome task   for any two bearers
though fearless and bold;   four had to carry
Grendel's great head   on a gory spear
to the well-decked hall—   a weary labor—
1640 until presently   proud warrior Geats,
bold, battle-keen,   neared the banquet-hall,
fourteen together,   their famous leader,
steadfast among them,   strode to the meadhall.
Then there entered in   the honored captain,
1645 daring in deeds,   deemed eminent,
a lion in battle,   to salute Hrothgar.
Then hauled by the hair   the head of Grendel
was dragged inside   where Danes were feasting.
It was loathsome to men   and to the lady there,
1650 yet a wondrous sight   that warriors gazed on.
XXIIII    Thus spoke then Beowulf,   born to Ecgtheow:
"Here, son of Halfdane,   happily we bring you
to express triumph   these spoils of the pool
that you look on here,   Lord of Scyldings.
1655 And yet I hardly survived   that hard-fought venture,
a work under water   in a wild combat.
Straightway the struggle   would have stopped outright
had God not granted   the gift of protection.
I could accomplish   in that conflict, naught
1660 with the blade Hrunting,   best of weapons;
but the Ruler of men   directed my attention
to a handsome glaive   hanging on a wall-rack,
ancient, enormous—   often He has guided
abandoned ones and friendless—   so that I brandished the
                                          sword.
1665 I killed in the conflict   when the occasion arrived
those who kept the cave.   Then that claymore burned
as the embellished blade   made blood spring forth,
hottest heart's blood.   With that hilt I returned
in the fiend's despite,   fatal slaughter
1670 and crimes requited   as was clearly right.

[ 65 ]

I then can promise   that you may plan to sleep
here in Heorot   happy, untroubled,
and with both tried and young   of your troop of men,
and every freeman Dane,   so you need fear nothing
1675   from the fen-dwellers   as before you did,
murderous manslaughter,   O mighty Scylding!"
     Then was the ancient hilt,   artwork of giants,
golden handgrip,   given the chieftain,
wise warleader;   it went to possession
1680   of the Danish king,   after the demon's fall,
wondrous work of wrights;   and when this world was left
by the fierce-minded   foe of the Godhead,
marked by murder,   and his mother too,
it passed to the power   of the people's king,
1685   best of monarchs   between broad oceans
of those who shared the wealth   in Scylding country.
     Hrothgar spoke then,   reading the markings
on the handsome hilt,   handed down from long past.
On it was etched the first   of ancient struggles
1690   when the driving flood   drowned the giants,
torment tore them;   to the eternal Lord
they were alien,   so the Almighty
had requited them   with covering waters.
Thus on the pommelplate   were placed rune-staves
1695   set in radiant gold   rightly graven,
written and recorded   for whom that rare weapon
with writhing reptiles   was wrought and embellished.
     Then the sage leader,   son of Halfdane,
said to the assembly   —they were silent all—:
1700   "Lo, one can tell you,   who upholds truth and right
for kin and clansmen,   recalling the whole past,
a chief and protector,   that this champion of ours
was worthiest of warriors.   Throughout wide regions
your fame is exalted,   my friend, Beowulf,
1705   even over every nation.   You managed all your power
with patience and prudence of spirit.   As I had proffered
                                         before now,
I shall fulfill our friendship.
                         "You shall be a future comfort,

[ 66 ]

long enduring    to your landsmen all,
and to heroes a help.    Not so was Heremod
1710    to Ecgwela's heirs,    the honored Scyldings.
He did not grow, make glad,    but brought grim carnage,
deadly damage    to Danish people.
In furious frenzy    he felled companions,
table comrades,    until he turned alone
1715    from delights of men,    an illustrious prince!
Although powerful God    placed him above
every other    in all privilege,
supported him in his power,    yet in his proud spirit
his soul grew savage.    He ceded no treasure
1720    to Danes for the glory,    but dismal he continued,
suffering sorely    from slow affliction
in that long struggle.    May you learn from that
to understand virtue.    This story I told you
from the wisdom of years.
                                        "Wonderful to tell you
1725    how through his ample heart    almighty God
strews statesmanship,    estates and valor
among the race of men;    He rules everything.
He may let the mind of a man    of mighty kindred
wander as he wishes,    grant him the world's pleasures
1730    in his homeland rule    of a haven for men,
regions of earth,    a realm limitless
be subject to him,    until he himself vainly
in his delusion believes    this will last to the end.
Abiding in abundance,    balked by nothing,
1735    neither illness nor age;    no evil afflictions
befoul his spirit,    nor feuds anywhere
reveal violence,    vicious hatred,
but the errant earth,    all that he touches
XXV    walks as he wishes;    of worse he knows nothing.
1740    But then within his breast    overweening
waxes and widens,    while the watchman sleeps,
the soul's sentinel.    Too sound that rest,
enmeshed in trouble,    the murderer near,
evilly aiming    an arrow from his bowstring.

1745 Then, though helmed, he is hit   in the heart sharply
with a shaft—unsure   how to shelter himself
from the perverse advice   of his vile demon.
What for long he held   seems too little for him.
No gold rings he gives out,   but, greedy and savage,
1750 cares not for honor,   nor the coming fate,
heedless, forgetful   of the host of rewards
the glorious Ruler,   God, dispensed before.
Finally again   it may befall at last
that the brief body   one bears may falter
1755 and fall fated;   fearless one seizes
the others' heirlooms,   unworried expending
the warrior's wealth   as he wishes to.
   "Fend off affliction,   my friend, Beowulf,
finest of men;   prefer the better—
1760 eternal gains;   turn from arrogance,
renowned champion!   You are known for strength
in your early youth,   but then all at once
swordblade or sickness   will sever you from power,
or the flames' embrace,   or the flood swelling,
1765 or the falchion's fall,   or the flight of a spear,
or loathsome age,   or the light of eyes
will falter and fail;   and at the first moment
death will crush you,   daring warrior.
   "A hundred seasons   I have held Denmark;
1770 beneath the skies I ruled   to exclude by war
many nations   throughout middle earth
with sword and spear   till 'neath the sweep of sky
I could name no one   nerved to oppose me.
Well, there came an upset for me   in my own country,
1775 grief after gaiety   on Grendel's coming,
an old enemy,   my obdurate intruder.
The ceaseless burden   of that pursuit I bore,
grave grief at heart.   To God eternal
be now thanks that I   have come through alive,
1780 after this old struggle   so my eyes may gaze
on that sword, bloodied,   and that dissevered head!
Join your comrades   and enjoy the feast,
war-honored one.   Waking tomorrow
we two shall share alike   the shower of treasures."

1785     With a happy heart   the hero of Weders
at once sought his seat   as the sage bade him.
Then again as before   for guests and followers,
famed for courage,   a feast was offered.
Deepening shadows,   dark above companions,
1790     neared as night came.   The nobles all arose;
the senior Scylding   would seek his bed.
The Geat too yearned deeply   to yield to rest,
the famous fighter   come from far away.
Promptly the attendant   with polished manners,
1795     one well aware   of a warrior's needs,
such as seafarers   sought to have then,
now ushered forth   the overtaxed defender.

      Then that great heart, too,   gave in to slumber.
The golden gabled   guest-hall towered
1800     above the sleeping guest,   who lay safe within,
until the blithe blackbird   sang the bliss of skies.
Then there came spreading   splendor of brightness
shining over shadows.   Shieldwarriors rushed,
princes were prone now   to depart again
1805     back to the people.   The bold visitor
wished to fare afar   in his faithful ship.

      Courageous Beowulf   had Hrunting borne
to Ecglaf's offspring,   asked him to take it,
that esteemed steelblade.   He bestowed his thanks
1810     for that loan, believed   a leal friend in war,
mighty in battle;   nor did he mention faults
in the hard-edged blade;   that was a high-souled man.
Impatient for departure,   prepared in armor,
the warriors waited.   He went to the highseat,
1815     a prince prized by Danes,   where sat the prudent Hrothgar;
the valiant victor   advanced to greet him.
XXVI     Beowulf spoke, then,   born to Ecgtheow:
"Now we seafarers,   sailors from a far land,
would like to say we desire   to seek Hygelac.
1820     We were entertained   as each might wish for;
we were well treated.   Warrior chieftain,
if I can earn on earth   by exploits of war
more of your affection,   I shall make ready
straightway to strive   in your stout defence.

1825　If I should hear again　across the huge ocean
　　　　hateful neighbors　send horror anew,
　　　　as at times they tried　attacking your household,
　　　　I shall bring a thousand thanes　against their threat of force,
　　　　heroes to help you.　As for Hygelac the prince,
1830　though young he be,　he is the Geats' leader,
　　　　guarding the people,　and I can guarantee
　　　　that by work and words　he will wish to help
　　　　so I may show esteem　and bring my shafted spear
　　　　and support of strength　to oppose the foe,
1835　hostile invaders,　helping where needed.
　　　　If then your son Hrethric　decides to visit
　　　　at the court of Geats,　he can count on friends
　　　　and will find many;　far-off acquaintance
　　　　is sought rightly　by one who himself is strong."
1840　　Hrothgar answered　readily saying:
　　　　"Surely the wise Master　sent those words and thoughts
　　　　that your heart uttered;　I have heard no man
　　　　who so early in life　ever seemed wiser.
　　　　You are in power strong,　prudent in spirit,
1845　sensible in speaking.　It seems to me likely,
　　　　if it happen, perhaps,　that hard-fought battle,
　　　　sickness or sword　or sailing spear-point
　　　　should slay the sons　of your sovereign lord,
　　　　leader of the people,　and you live after,
1850　that the Battle-Geats　will have no better man
　　　　than you* to choose as king,　chief, and guardian
　　　　of the warriors' wealth,　if you wish to hold
　　　　your kinsman's kingdom.　Your clear thinking
　　　　I admire the more　as your mind is known,
1855　my cherished Beowulf.　You have achieved for us,
　　　　for Weders and West-Danes,　warmest friendship;
　　　　wars and feuding,　waged earlier on,
　　　　are quelled and quarrels　are quieted fully.
　　　　While I wield control　in this wide kingdom
1860　there shall be joint treasures　enjoyed by giving
　　　　when good men greet us　across the gannet's bath.

The curving vessel    shall carry gifts
across the northern sea.    I know those people,
with friend and foe,    firm and steadfast,
1865    all innocent    in the old manner."
        Thereupon Halfdane's son,    heroes' defender,
had him take treasures,    twelve more presents,
and seek in safety    with these signs of love
his own dear people,    but make an early return.
1870    The head of Scyldings,    a highborn ruler,
then embraced and kissed    the best of retainers,
and as he clasped him close    coursing teardrops
fell from the frost-haired chief.    He faced two prospects,
as a wise ancient,    one he expected:
1875    that they would meet no more    in meadhall or council
where the daring sat.    He was so dear a friend
that the king could not    calm his heart's tumult,
though he hid his longing    for the loved hero,
it burned in his blood,    bound in his heartstrings
1880    as his breast's burden.    Beowulf departed
across the grassy ground,    a gold-decked warrior,
elated by the riches.    The long voyager
rode at anchor    ready for its master.
On the road seaward    Hrothgar's good gifts
1885    were often praised.    He was an unequaled king,
utterly blameless    until age robbed him
of strength and its pleasures,    as it destroys many.
XXVII        Then there came to the coast    in a company
courageous youths    in ringmail corslets,
1890    linked limbcover.    The look-out noticed
the troop returning    when they attained the land.
He did not greet the guests    with neglect or harm
from the crest of the cliff,    but cantered toward them,
said the bright-mailed band    embarking below
1895    would be welcome    to the Weder folk.
Then on the sandy shore    to the sea-vessel
with its curving prow    was carted armor,
mounts and massive treasure;    the mast rose above
Hrothgar's bounty,    riches and war-gear.

1900 Then the captain gave    to him who kept boatguard
a blade bound with gold;    on the bench in hall
he was held after    of higher honor
for that grand heirloom.
                                    The good ship set forth,
left the land of Danes,    launched on the deep.
1905 Then like a sea garment    the sail was fastened
to the mast with rope;    moaning timbers
nor yet wind over wave    worked to hinder
the vessel's journey.    The voyager sped
with foam at prow    forth across the water,
1910 its curved stem cutting    the currents below,
till the cliffs appeared    and coastal headlands,
sheltered shores of home.    The ship, wind-driven,
bore swiftly on    and beached on the shingle.
The watch at the harbor    at once was ready.
1915 He had looked for long    for the loved warriors
far on the currents    of the flowing tide.
The broad-beamed vessel    he bound fast on sands
with anchor hawsers,    lest the ocean's force
should wash away    the well-formed timbers.
1920 He had the prince's wealth    transported with them,
ornaments and armor;    the unstinting lord,
Hygelac of Geats,    had his home nearby,
set by the seacliff    with his assembled thanes.
Noble the stronghold,    renowned the ruler,
1925 high placed in hall;    Hygd young and wise,
most accomplished,    though not many years
had this court enclosed    this kindly lady,
Haereth's daughter;    yet she held back naught,
gave generously    gifts of treasure.
1930 Not hers the pride of Thryth,    imperious queen,
who called for crimes    of cruel violence;
none so valiant and bold    among devoted comrades
as to dare by day    to endanger himself,
but her lord alone    would look upon her
1935 or he might hold for sure    that hand-twisted bonds,
deadly fetters,    were destined for him.

Quickly after capture    it was decreed a sword
with embellished blade    would bring his end
and report to the people    of his penalty.
1940    No queenly custom    for courtly practice,
though she should peerless be,    that a peacemaker
demand the lifeblood    for imagined wrong
by a well-loved man,    an unworthy deed.
Yet Hemming's kinsman    hindered that conduct.
1945    Those ale-drinking    spread other tales,
that the injuries,    acts hostile, too,
faced future change    since she first had gone,
given goldbedecked,    graced with virtues,
to the young hero    when yonder she journeyed
1950    over furrowed flood*    at father's counsel
to Offa's castle.    There she after found
fate fitted her,    famed for merit,
holding the throne    highly honored;
long love she kept    for the lord of warriors.
1955    They say of all mankind    he was honored most
from sea to sea,    excelling others,
widely regarded    for his wars and gifts,
the bounteous Offa,    a bold fightingman,
held his homeland    hardily and wisely.
1960    In time his son, Eomor,    served in combat,
a help to heroes,    Hemming's kinsman,
grandson of Garmund.

XXVIII                                    Then along gleaming sands
the lord and leader    led his comrades
on the broad beaches.    Bright sunlight glowed;
1965    the sun beamed from the south.    They set their way,
hastening forward    where they heard the king,
bane of Ongentheow,    bulwark of men,
a daring war-king,    was dealing out arm-rings
in the hall of the fort.    Hygelac was told
1970    quickly that his nephew    was coming to greet him;
Beowulf the defender,    bearing his shield
had come unharmed, alive,    from high games of war
and was entering    the outer courtyard.

Promptly place was cleared    for the approaching guests
1975  as the mighty chief    commanded his liegemen,
so that all could sit    within on alebenches.
    He who came safe from strife    sat opposite;
kinsman faced kinsman;    after his courteous words
greeted graciously    his own great leader.
1980  Haereth's daughter,    holding meadcups,
circled through the assembly,    considerate and kindly,
carried cups of drink    to the company.
Then from that high seat    Hygelac proceeded
to question his comrade,    courteous and eager,
1985  curious to discover    the course of the venture
that the Sea-Geats sought    when they sailed away.
"What chanced on the journey,    cherished Beowulf,
when on a sudden    you decided to cross
the sea to succor    besieged Hart afar
1990  intent on battle?    Those troubles so well known,
did you then remedy    for Hrothgar, our ally,
the famous leader?    I have reflected much,
anxious at heart,    agitated,
doubting the venture    of my dear kinsman.
1995  'Leave him alone!'    I had long begged you
not to meet in strife    that murderous stranger,
but let Danes themselves    deal with Grendel.
That I see you safe    I send thanks to God."
    Beowulf answered,    born to Ecgtheow:
2000  "That is clear to men,    my King Hygelac,
famous the fighting.    What a fray was ours,
Grendel's and mine,    in that great meadhall,
where he had meted out    misery to Scyldings,
sorrows unceasing    centered on Heorot,
2005  uninterrupted!    All I avenged,
so Grendel's mother    need not gloat ever
at that din at dawn,    though her days extend
longest in life    of that loathsome race,
enmeshed in malice.    I first made my way
2010  to that great stronghold    to greet there Hrothgar;
at once Halfdane's son,    high and famous,
set me near his sons    when he knew my mind,

[ 74 ]

assigning a seat there.   I have seen nowhere
hallguests happier   under heaven's vault,
2015 in mead more pleasure,   a merrier gathering.   .
The people's peace-bond,   that peerless queen,
urged on the youths   all through the hall.
Often she offered   armbands and buckles
to the fighting men   before she found her seat.
2020 Sometimes before ranked veterans   Hrothgar's daughter
brought the ale flagon   to each in turn.
Men in the meadhall   mentioned Freawaru
as she handed round   the handsome goblet
to the picked heroes.   She is the promised bride
2025 a girl, gold-adorned,   to gracious Ingeld;
that was arranged before   by the realm's guardian,
King of Scyldings.   He counts it prudent
that feuds and fighting   find settlement
by means of this maiden.   And yet more often,
2030 after the death of a prince   the deadly spearpoint
lingers but little,   though the lady be choice.
      It may displease the prince,   proud Heathobard,
and the tribal thanes   when he treads the floor
with the dear maiden:   Danish youngsters
2035 treated as nobles;   treasured heirlooms,
glaives and falchions   glistening on thigh,
hard, hung by rings,   that the Heathobards
once had wielded,   weapons of fame
until their lives were lost   to deluded hopes
2040 and the shock of shields   shattered their comrades.
XXVIIII Beholding the hilt-ring   a hoary spearman,
who remembers all,   mournful at heart
at that spear-slaughter,   speaks at the banquet.
Despondent in spirit   he explores the mind,
2045 waking to war   a willing champion
through his inner thoughts,   and he utters this:
      "My comrade, can you   recall that falchion,
the excellent iron   that your own father
bore to battle,   bravely armored,
2050 in his final fight   where he was felled by Danes,
the hardy Scyldings,   who held the field
when, after warriors fell,   Withergyld perished?

[ 75 ]

Now here some callous child   of these killers struts,
gloating in his gear   in the great chamber,
2055 boasts of the slaying,   bearing the treasure
you should have held rightly   as your heritage.
He stirs him and steels him   with stinging reminders
on many occasions   until the moment comes
that the lady's thane   lies drenched in blood
2060 from a stroke of steel   struck down in a feud,
forfeiting life   for his father's guilt;
his foe flees the land,   informed of its pathways.
Both will be breaking   bound oaths given,
sworn words severed.   Then will surging hate
2065 enter Ingeld;   interest in his lady
and love will lessen   with lingering trouble.
Therefore I hold hollow   those Heathobards'
lordly alliance   with loyal Danes,
a specious friendship.
                                   "Now I shall speak further
2070 again of Grendel   that you may grasp in full,
O treasure-giver,   the turn of matters
in the hand fighting.   After heaven's gem
glided over grasslands   the grim spirit came,
savage in twilight,   seeking booty,
2075 where we held the hall,   unharmed and ready.
His assault on Hart   slew there Handscioh;
it was a deadly doom   by which he died the first,
a girded warrior.   Grendel was slayer
of the glorious thane,   gulping the body
2080 of that dear fellow,   indulging his greed.
Yet he would not agree to go   from that golden hall
eagerly eating   but empty-handed.
His mind was set on murder,   his mouth, bloody-toothed;
but distinguished for strength,   he strove to test me,
2085 and grasped greedily.   A great pouch hung there,
cunningly closed   with peculiar hooks;
arts of devils   and able invention
had prepared the pouch   from pelts of dragons.

He would add me in    to other victims,
2090    though I was innocent.    The evil-doer
would have many a meal.    But that might not be
when I stood upright,    angry, defiant.
Too long is the telling    how I returned his crimes,
his endless evils,    to the injurer.
2095    There, my prince, I proved    your people's honor
by my worthy works.    He got away safely
to the delights of life    for a little while,
yet his right hand stayed    as relic in Heorot,
and saddened, downcast,    he then slunk away,
2100    dropping to the darkness    of the deep waters.
XXX        For that fatal fight    the friendly Scylding
gave me a princely price    in plated goldwork
and many treasures    after morning came
and we joined the Danes    enjoying the feast.
2105    There were sagas and songs;    a senior Scylding,
questioned, recalling    curious stories.
The battle-brave one    brought men delight.
At times he touched    the tuneful harpstrings,
sometimes telling tales,    true and sorrowful,
2110    or strange stories.    The stout-hearted king
told truly and well;    at times again
a warrior, bowed by years,    would bewail his youth
and his battle strength.    His breast heaved within
when he remembered much,    mind agèd, wise.
2115        So all day long    inside Heorot
we knew delight    until night approached.
Grendel's mother    again was ready
for a swift vengeance,    sad voyager;
she sought the slayers    of her son, murdered
2120    in fierce fray with Geats.    The frightful woman
then avenged her son,    viciously slaying
a warrior of might,    the wise councillor,
old Ashhere,    who gave up his life.
The men of Denmark    after morning came
2125    might not burn blazing    the best of liegemen,
nor feed the fallen    to the funeral pyre.

Bearing the body    she brought it under
the falling waters    in her fiend's embrace.
That was for Hrothgar    the rawest anguish
2130    of those the lord of Danes    had long suffered.
    Then that prince implored me    by your precious life,
to work worthy deeds    in the wave's tumult,
risking my life    and reaping glory;
he would reward me well.    As is widely known,
2135    I found in the flood    a fierce and dreadful
keeper of the chasm.    In close handbattle
we fought with fury    unflinching a while;
waves welled with gore    in that wan dwelling;
with huge hilted blade    I beheaded the dam,
2140    mother of Grendel.    Not yet marked for death
I scarcely succeeded    in escaping alive,
but the soldiers' saver,    son of Halfdane
made me gifts again    of gear and riches.

XXXI    Thus lived the nation's king    by noble customs;
2145    I had missed no part    of the meed promised,
prize for my prowess,    but he proffered wealth
of my own choosing,    heir to Halfdane.
These, my warleader,    I wish to bring you,
offered in honor.    Yet all favors
2150    now fall to you.    I have few but you
as my close kinsman,    kindest Hygelac."
    Then he had brought inside    the boar's head standard,
the high helmet for war,    hauberk of gray,
costly claymore,    and recounted his tale:
2155    "This rich war-gear    Hrothgar gave me;
the keen commander    then requested me
to tell you truly    of his treasured gifts.
He said it had been carried    by King Heregar,
lord of Scyldings;    long he had owned it,
2160    but he was loath to leave    that linked corslet
to his own offspring,    able Hereward,
though a loyal son.    Luck attend it!"
    I heard that four horses,    in fleetness alike,
matched dappled bays*    remained with the trappings.

2165 Steeds and riches   he bestowed on the king.
So ought kin to do,   not kindle malice
by secret skill,   nor send to death
his close comrades.   He had kept the faith
with Hygelac his prince,   hardy in battle;
2170 each with careful regard   for his kin's welfare:
So should a sister's son   who sought his uncle.
I heard he tendered the torque,   the treasured marvel,
as a gift to Hygd,   given him by Wealhtheow,
a prince's daughter,   with a present of steeds,
2175 high-stepping horses   with handsome saddles.
Then was her breast adorned   the better with the necklace.
    Thus did Ecgtheow's son   exemplify honor,
known for battles   and for noble deeds.
He behaved fairly,   harmed no drinkers,
2180 killed no comrades.   His was no cruel heart:
a fearless fighter,   he kept in full the gift
that God had granted,   the greatest vigor
man could be given.   Many despised him;
young Geats thought him   a youth unready
2185 nor would his chief choose him   for choice bounty
in the feasting hall.   Him they firmly believed
a passive prince,   unpromising,
a slothful soldier.   But a sudden change
from former affliction   came to that famous man.*
2190     Then the bulwark of men,   battle-famous king,
directed to bring him   Hrethel's heirloom—
there was no better blade,   embellished with goldwork,
no truer treasure,   entrusted to Weders.
He had them bring Beowulf   the brand, laying it
2195 in his lap; he allowed   liberal holdings,
hall and high seat.   Inherited landrights
both might claim to hold   in that countryside,
home and homestead;   to the higher ranked
went a broad kingdom   and bounteous riches.

# The Last Victory:
## THE DRAGON AND DEATH

2200      Afterwards, later   in loud clash of war
       Hygelac had fallen   and Heardred been slaughtered
       below the shield-shelter   by sharp claymores,
       death-dealing blades,   when daring Swedes,
       fierce fightingmen,   found him by seeking
2205      among his honored Geats   and with enmity
       hunted and harried   Hereric's nephew;
       afterwards the broad kingdom   passed to Beowulf's hand.
       For fifty years   he defended it well.
       He held the homelands   as head of the nation,
2210      wise and worthy,   until the wyrm arose,
       a dragon ruling   in the dark night-time
       the heath-covered height   as the hoardwatcher
       on the stony steep.   A strait track led there,
       hidden, unheeded.   But some human wretch
2215      at last entered in   even to the treasure,
       heaped by heathens;   his hand grasped a cup,
       broad, bright with gems.   Nor did the beast conceal
       that it was deceived in sleep   by the sleights of a thief.
       Neighboring folk   knew its trouble
2220      when tribal troops   felt its intense fury.
XXXII      It was not his aim nor end   nor by his own wishes
       that he who did bitter wrong   broke into the treasure;
       but in sore distress   the slave of a warrior
       fled from a flogging   and would find shelter,
2225      and so crept inside,   conscious of guilt.
       Struck with stark fear,   the stranger noticed
       the sinuous serpent,   yet the sorry wretch
       departed the peril,   made a prompt exit.
       When the sudden assault   descended on him
2230      he clutched quickly   a costly beaker.
       In that earthen cave   ancient treasures
       had been hoarded of old,   hidden by others,

ample heirlooms    of an honored race,
precious riches    prudently preserved
2235 in dark depths of earth    till the destined hour.
Death dragged them off    in days departed,
and he who lived longest    of loyal comrades,
a guardian grieving    at the grave of friends,
looked for a like fate    to alight on him,
2240 that but a little while    he'd be allowed to hold
that brave treasure.    A barrow stood ready,
freshly fashioned    with confined access
by breaking billows    and beetling headland.
Thither the gold-keeper    gathered riches,
2245 well-hoarded wealth    of warrior chieftains,
fretted armor;    a few words he spoke:
"Ground, now guard you    goods of nobles
since heroes cannot.    Here once within you
good men got it;    grim death took off,
2250 dangerous and deadly,    each dear comrade,
kinsmen of mine    who closed their eyes
having seen sweet days.    My sword none carries
nor polishes    the plated flagon,
the cherished chalice.    Champions vanish.
2255 That hard helmet    must lose hammered gold,
deprived of plating;    those who should polish it,
burnishers of beavers,    are bowed in death.
Even so that corslet    in combat suffered
above the shock of shields    sharp blows of swords
2260 moulders with its master;    nor can the mail hauberk
wander widely    with the war-leader
at the soldier's side.    No song of harpers,
merry music,    nor moor-bred falcon
wings through the winehall,    nor warhorse stamping
2265 in the castle court.    The cold hand of death
with savage slaughter    cut down souls enough!"
     Thus alone the last    after lost comrades
roamed wretchedly,    wrung by sorrow
daytime and night-time    until death's tumult
2270 touched and tore his heart.    A twilight menace
discovered uncared for    costly treasures;

a dreaded dragon   who darts forth by night,
bare and burning   to barrows, searching,
flame enfolded,   feared by earthdwellers.
2275 Hidden hoards it seeks,   all that heathen wealth,
and it guards the gold,   grown wise in years,
yet not a bit better   for that buried hoard.
      Thus that threat to men   three hundred years
guarded the storehouse,   great chambered hold
2280 in the earth below,   until one angered it
when the carl carried   the cup to his master,
who took as a pledge of peace   the plated beaker,
liegeman to lord.   So much less the hoard,
its ring-store plundered   and the wretched man
2285 accorded clemency.   His captain examined
for the first time crafts   of former ages.
      Then that wyrm awoke,   woe rose anew;
resolute it wriggled   along the rock to find
where the stranger stepped   in stealthy cunning;
2290 he had come too close   to the coiled dragon.
So can undoomed ones   easily win through
ill luck and exile   when the Almighty's
favor defends them!   Furiously prowling
the treasure-protector   tracked along the surface,
2295 hunting the human   who harmed it sleeping.
Fierce and fiery   it went forth circling
about the knoll outside.   No one walked there
on that wild wasteland,   yet in war it rejoiced
and battle action.   Within the barrow it searched
2300 to find the flagon;   it knew finally
that some man managed   to meddle with its gold-hoard,
plate and precious gems.   Impatiently
the hoard-protector   awaited hiding dusk.
The barrow-keeper   boiled with anger;
2305 now it would proffer   payment in flames
for the drinking-cup.   Then the day ended
as the snake desired;   it slipped from the earthwork,
lingering no longer,   and lunged, breathing fire,
enfolded in flame.   Thus it first began,
2310 fearful to the folk   and fatal later
to their gold-giver   at the grievous end.

XXXIII      Then the beast's belly    belched forth embers,
burned bright dwellings.    The blazing radiance
struck horror at heart.    The hated monster
2315 would leave none living.    Ever near and far
its feverish fighting,    its fierce malice
were widely noticed;    how the winging scourge
hated and humbled    the hearts of Weders
with stark destruction.    Straightway at dawn
2320 to the hidden hoard    it hastened flying.
With flame it enfolded    the unfortunate men
in a burning blaze;    the barrow it trusted,
walls and warfare;    wanhope it proved.
     Then was Beowulf brought    the bare truth promptly,
2325 dread and danger    to his dear stronghold—
the best of buildings    in the blaze melted
with the chair of choice.    Then that champion
was strongly disturbed    by distress at heart.
The wise man wondered    if the World Ruler,
2330 the eternal Lord,    were truly angry
at a broken law.    His breast was in tumult
from clouded forebodings,    an unaccustomed mood.
     With its burning coals    the blazing dragon
had destroyed outright    the stronghold of the people
2335 from the coast inland.    The king of Weders
then devised revenge,    a valiant ruler.
The lord of fightingmen,    leader of warriors,
ordered fashioned    an iron war-shield,
wondrously worked,    for he well perceived
2340 that no wood of the weald    wards off fire-breath;
flame feeds on shields.    Faring from daylight*
the prince, proved of old,    was to depart the world
and endure his end—    the dragon also,
though it had held for long    the hoarded treasures.
2345      The prince, ring-giver,    then repulsed the thought
that the far-flier    be sought with fighting men
in full force of troops.    Fearless of battle
he looked for little    from the loathed dragon
in vigor or valor    as a violent foe,

2350 for he had braved battle   and many bold assaults,
clashes of combat,   since cleansing the hall
in the land of Danes.   A lucky winner,
in encounters he crushed   the kindred of Grendel,
a loathsome family.   Not the least of trials,
2355 that hard hand-meeting   when Hygelac fell,
his friendly leader,   famed lord of Geats,
Hrethel's offspring;   in the rush of war
bloody blades slew him   butchered by a sword stroke
on the Friesian shore.   Finally Beowulf
2360 succeeded in escaping   by his swimming skill;
thirty thanes' war-gear   his thews supported*
as he turned seaward.   The tribe of Hetware
had no grounds to gloat,   engage in battle,
bringing their bucklers   boldly forward;
2365 from that fightingman   few came away
and sought their homes.   The son of Ecgtheow
swam swelling waves   across the sea homeward,
forlorn, alone   to his land and folk.
Hygd there offered   hoard and kingdom,
2370 rings and royal throne.   She could not rest assured
her son could safeguard   the ancestral throne
against foreigners,   since his father's death.
That deprived people's   pleas were in vain
that the highborn chief   be Heardred's ruler,
2375 or accept and assume   the sovereignty.
Yet he supported the prince,   his people's leader,
with fealty, favor,   and friendly counsel,
till older and abler   he had earned control
of the warlike Geats.   Across the waves approached
2380 outcast exiles,   Ohthere's sons,
seeking Heardred,   insurgent rebels
against the Swedish king,   a sea-king of note,
shield of Scylfings,   sharer of treasure,
a most mighty prince.   He was marked for death
2385 when for that friendship   by a fatal wound
from a brandished blade   the boy-prince perished.
Ongentheow's offspring,   Onela departed,
heading homeward   after Heardred's death;

that kingly Beowulf  might then claim the throne
2390 and so guide the Geats.  He was a good ruler!
XXXIIII    Then in later days,  his lord's death recalled,
he planned repayment,  and proffered Eadgils
friendship in need.  His forces supported
Ohthere's son  with arms and men
2395 across the wide water.  Later he won revenge,
killing the king  after care-plagued raids.
      Thus till now surviving  every violence,
savage assault,  sought-for exploit,
until that certain day  the son of Ecgtheow
2400 fought to the finish  with that fire-dragon.
Then as one of twelve  the warlord of Geats
stood, stirred by wrath,  to study the dragon;
he had found by then  whence the feud arose,
malice to mankind.  By means of an informer
2405 the famous flagon  had fallen to his coffers.
The thirteenth fellow,  the thief of the cup—
he who had started the strife—  now stepped forth leading.
He was a sorry slave,  sad, disheartened,
and must guide the group.  He went against his will
2410 up to the earthhall;  an entrance he knew.
Turf topped the mound  by tumult of breakers
and the surging sea,  and inside lay heaps
of artwork and inlay.  An odious keeper,
watchful and war-eager,  held the wealthy hoard,
2415 old under earth.  That was no easy gain
for any champion  to achieve by arms.
He sat on the headland,  the hardy fighter,
gold-giver of Geats,  greeted his comrades,
hoped health to all.  Yet his heart was sad,
2420 restless but ready,  as he reached near death,
which must confront and face  that fine old leader,
hunt his heart's treasure,  halve asunder
breath and body;  the brave prince's flesh
would no more swaddle soul,  soon departing.
2425    Beowulf held forth,  born to Ecgtheow:
"Many a stark struggle  have I withstood in youth,
times of trouble;  I can tell it all.

When my rich ruler,   royal friend of Geats,
sent to my father,   I was but seven years.
2430 But my King Hrethel   kept me and reared me,
gave me fortune, feasts,   favor of our kinship.
He did not like me less   by the least portion,
a lad in his landhold,   than his loved children,
Herebald and Hathcyn   or Hygelac, my leader.
2435 For that eldest one,   unfittingly,
a cruel couch was spread   by a kinsman's deed
after Hathcyn's hand   on the horned longbow
let fly a feathered shaft   that struck his friendly lord,
missing the mark,   a mortal error;
2440 with a bloody bolt   brother slew other.
Unredressed that deed,   deep wrong festered,
heart-heavy pain;   yet the high-born prince
had to lose his life,   to the last unatoned.
      "Such is the ache of heart   an old man suffers,
2445 bowed down bearing   that his boy dangles
young on the gibbet.   Then he yearns aloud
a sadhearted song   when his son is hanging
for the carrion crows,   no cure, no vengeance.
The old can offer   his own no solace.
2450 Ever he remembers   as morning wakens
how he lost the lad.   He looks for no other,
no second son   to succeed to him
as an heir for his age,   when his only son,
doomed to the deathride,   plumbed the depths of life.
2455 He sees in sorrow   his son's chambers,
winehall now waste,   windswept pallet,
and the gladness gone.   The grave has the rider,
the soldier sleeping.   No sound of a harper,
no more games on the green,   nor the glee of yore.
XXXV 2460 Then he mounts to rest   mourning alone
for his only child;   they seem all too wide,
those idle acres,   that empty room.
      "Thus the guard of Geats,   grief at heart welling,
for his Herebald,   harbored anguish.
2465 He could not relieve the loss,   lash out at the slayer,
and so injure an heir   who had aimed badly,
though for the deadly deed   he was dear no more.

[ 87 ]

Then in that sorrow, which sorely rankled,
he chose the love of the Lord not delight of men.
2470 As fits the prosperous, at his passing he left,
ceded to descendants seizin and townships.

"Then came storm and strife, stinging rancor,
over the wide water by both Weders and Swedes,
wrought in common after Hrethel fell;
2475 for still Ongentheow's offspring remained,
bold and battle-keen, bent on no friendship
across the inland sea, and often committed
raw red carnage about Hreosnabeorh.
My friends and family sought full vengeance
2480 for enmity and evils, just as all were aware,
although the prince himself paid with his lifeblood—
a bitter bargain. But the brave leader,
Hathcyn, the Geat, paid heavily.
Then in the morning I learned murder was requited
2485 when with burnished blade brother met slayer
as Ongentheow sought Eofor's life;
warhelm split wide, the wily Scylfing
dropped deathly pale. Debts of slaughter
the heart remembered and withheld no blow.

2490 "I returned treasure tendered me by Hygelac
by my efforts of arms and acts of valor
with my bright broadsword in the brunt of war,
as my lot allowed; lands he had granted,
holding and home. He would hardly need
2495 to seek over Sweden or South Danes and Gifthas
for some worse warrior who wanted payment
since alone in the lead I led his soldiers;
and thus while life shall last I shall no less struggle,
my steel standing firm, for that staunch weapon
2500 aided me ever and was often drawn
since I dealt the death to that Dayraven,
a Frankish fighter, before my friends in arms.
He brought no fresh treasure to the Friesian king,
breast ornaments not one brought away;
2505 bowed down in battle was the banner guard,
a prince in his power. Point nor edge slew him;

his breast was broken    and its beating stilled
in a battlegrip.    Now must blade of steel,
hand and hard sword,    over the hoard battle."
2510    Beowulf spoke out,    brave words uttering
in this final hour:    "When I was first in arms
I dared many dangers,    still I seek deeds of worth
as tried protector,    turning to battle,
fighting for fame,    if that fire-dragon
2515    will seek me outside    his earthen hall."
Then for a last farewell    to his loved comrades
the hardy helmbearer    hailed each warrior,
his bosom fellows:    "No blade would I carry,
sword against the serpent,    if I could see my way
2520    in other action    unarmed to grapple
with that grim dragon,    as once with Grendel by hand.
Here I expect burning breath,    baneful destruction,
and pungent poison;    hence I approach wearing
breastmail and buckler.    Nor shall I budge a step
2525    from the gravemound's guard;    but how the Guide of men
favors our fate,    we must find at the wall.
Keen in courage    I decline to boast
against that war-flier.    Wait for me on the barrow,
you mail-coated men,    in your mesh hauberks;
2530    you will see full soon    after the assault is made
who best survives    our bitter conflict
of two contenders.    Nor is that task for you
nor any man's duty    except mine alone,
against the monster's might    to match his vigor,
2535    show his manliness.    By might of arms
I must win that wealth    or war will take me,
dealing your leader    deadly evil."
The famous fighter,    fierce in his helmet,
bore his battleshirt    bending in the entrance
2540    under the stony cliff.    Strength he trusted,
though but a single man's;    that is no slacker's way.
Vested with virtues    he had survived warfare
and crash of combat    when companies fought.
He saw along the rampart    rocky arches
2545    and from the barrow burst    a boiling torrent.

All that spurting spate    spouted flaming
with hot hostile fire,    hampering approach.
None could endure the depths    for the dragon's flames
uninjured, unscalded,    for any while.
2550    In a burst of anger    there broke a shout;
the raging roar issued    as the ruler of Geats,
stout-hearted, stormed.    His strong voice entered,
robust, ringing    under wraith-gray stone.
Wrath was aroused    when the rude keeper
2555    heard a human voice.    Here was no moment
to favor friendship.    Forth came at once
the beast's breath flaming    in burning fury
out from the entrance.    The earth resounded.
The bold one beneath the barrow,    brave chief of Geats,
2560    swung the disk of his shield    toward the dread serpent.
Then was the coiled creature    by courage enflamed
to fix on fighting.    The fearless war-king
first drew his falchion,    a famous heirloom
with a bitter blade.    Bent on slaughter
2565    each to other    was an awesome foe.
Stout-hearted he stopped    by his sturdy shield,
lord of loved comrades—    in loops the dragon
quickly coiled itself—    in his corslet he stood.
Then went the burning beast,    bending and curling,
2570    darting toward doom.    The dense shield guarded
life and limb safely,    but not so long a while
as the well-known prince    had wished protection.
Then first he found    fate denied him;
he might not manage    more fame in battle.
2575    The high chief of Geats    hewed with his weapon,
struck the stained terror    with the steel heirloom,
so the burnished blade    bent and faltered,
biting bone awry,    the blow much weaker
than the noble lord    had need of then,
2580    hardpressed, harried.    Then was the hoard-keeper,
after that battle blow    in a brutal mood,
flinging his flames.    The fire of battle
flared far and wide.    The friend of Weders
did not vaunt victory.    Vainly the war-sword
2585    was bared in battle;    its blade, long trusted,

failed for the first time.  That was no facile course
as Ecgtheow's heir,   the honored leader,
would leave the land,   look for a home
elsewhere than inside   these earthly bounds:
2590 so must everyone,   the end approaching,
leave his loan of days.  It was not long to then
when the combatants   encountered again.
The hoard-guard took heart   and with heaving breath
hastened forward.  He who once headed the folk
2595 sorely suffered,   encircled by flames.
Not at all his henchmen,   heroes' children,
closed their company   about the king in need
with warriors' honor,   but to the wood turning
saved themselves there.  But a single heart
2600 swelled with sorrow:   naught can swerve from kin
him who is right-minded   and reasonable.
XXXVI     Wiglaf, the warrior,   was Wihstan's son,
and a prized comrade,   prince of Scylfings,
Alfhere's kin.  He saw his overlord
2605 hardpressed by heat   under his helm of war.
He thought of honors   earlier given:
the wealthy homestead   of the Waymundings,
every family claim   that his father owned.
He could not hesitate;   hand gripped buckler,
2610 he bared his broadsword,   a blade long famous,
heirloom of Eanmund,   Ohtere's son.
On the field of war   the friendless exile
had fallen before Wihstan   at the falchion's bite.
He carried to his kinsman   corslet of ringmail,
2615 bright burnished helm,   that blade of giants.
Onela, the uncle,   paid him armor and gear,
fine furnishings,   when he felled Eanmund.
Nor did he vow vengeance   for the violence
that bowed in battle   his brother's son.
2620 He kept those furnishings   not a few seasons,
brand and breastmail,   until his boy could fight
like his forefathers   with foremost prowess.
Then among the Weders   war-gear he gave him
all unreckoned;   when old and wise
2625 he took leave of life.  At this latest hour

must the warrior youth    withstand war's onslaught
beside his friend and prince.    That was his first exploit.
His courage did not quaver    nor his kinsman's gift
weaken in warfare.    That the wyrm found out
2630    when he met those men    in the mound's passage.
        In well-chosen words    Wiglaf admonished
the laggard liegemen,    though forlorn of mood.
"I remember the meal    when after mead-drinking
we had promised our prince,    who had proffered arms
2635    there in the banquet-hall    that blades and helmets
would reward his trust    should he want for help.
Thereupon he chose us to serve,    the choice from his army,
for this armed action    of his own accord
recalling our courage    in his company
2640    on expeditions,    and offered these treasures
for he counted us keen    as we cast javelins,
eager in our armor—    though our overlord,
the troops' protector,    intended to enter
on this last exploit    alone, unaided,
2645    since he had done more deeds    of daring and glory
than other warriors.
                        "Now has the hour arrived
that our leader and lord    looks for the power
of worthy warriors.    Let us willingly
help our high captain    while heat afflicts him,
2650    grim, glowing flame!    God knows I'd choose
that my body bear    the blazing wildfire
along with my gold-giver    in that glaring heat.
It seems to me wrong indeed    that we reach our homes,
shield on shoulder,    unless we can shelter our prince
2655    and defeat his foe.    Full well I know
his early exploits    earned no misfortune,
and of seasoned Geats,    he was not singled out
to face affliction,    fall in battle.
We fight as fellows,    defenses we share,
2660    brand and battledress,    breastmail and helm."
        Into the fatal fumes    he followed his captain,
wearing his warhelm,    and some words he spoke:
"Belovèd Beowulf,    luck attend you!
as of yore you said,    young and eager,

[ 92 ]

2665 that as long as you lived   you'd allow nothing
of your fame to fail.   Now, unflinching prince,
well known for war-deeds,   work to your utmost
to hold safe your life;   I shall help you strive!"
        After those words that wyrm   in waves of flame
2670 loathsome, malicious,   lurched forth again;
it hunted the hated   human attackers.
Burned to the boss,   the broad shield crumbled,
nor could hauberk help   the hardy spearman,
but the young cousin,   yare and daring,
2675 covered by his king's shield   cast his off bravely
for embers had eaten   his own away.
But the king recalled   combats and glory,
and struck with such strength   that his stout broadsword,
forced by his fury,   fixed in the headplate.
2680 Beowulf's Naegling   broke asunder.
That falchion proved faulty,   failed him in battle,
a gray graven sword.   He was not granted help
from that old heirloom   with its iron blade.
His hand struck too hard,   as I have heard men say,
2685 too much it demanded   at each mighty blow
from the blades he bore;   they were blood-hardened,
but overstrained by his strokes;   his strength was useless.
        Then for a third attempt,   thinking of vengeance,
the frightful fire-drake,   foe of the people,
2690 charged the champion   when the chance arose.
Searing and savage,   it seized all his throat
in its tearing teeth.   A torrent of life-blood
welled from the warrior;   its waves bloodied him.
XXXVII      I have heard recounted   how, at his king's trouble,
2695 the shieldwarrior next him   showed his vigor,
his courage and keenness,   that came by nature.
He did not heed the head,   his hand was blistered
as he assisted his lord   and slashed the dragon
deeper down beneath.   Dense scales parted;
2700 the thane in armor   thrust his sword in,
blood-stained, embellished,   and the blaze began
to subside and sink.   Yet still, his senses aware,

the dazed king drew out    the deadly knife
carried on his corslet,    and cut the serpent
2705 swiftly at its center.    They slew the dragon,
courage overcoming    the creature's spirit,
kindred nobles    killed it together.
Such is a loyal thane    when his lord has need,
trustworthy, true.
                              That triumph for the leader
2710 was the last labor    of his life on earth.
Then began to smart and swell    with serpent's venom
the painful puncture    by the poison fangs.
Straightway he noticed    that there stirred within
that virulent venom    invading his breast,
2715 an anguished aching.    Then the old king went
lost deep in thought,    to a ledge by the wall.
He stopped to study    the structure of giants,
how the timeless tomb    contained within it
strong stone arches,    stable on their columns.
2720 Most worthy Wiglaf    washed his kinsman,
the battle-weary,    blood-stained chieftain.
He laved the leader,    the belovèd prince,
with friendly fingers    and unfastened his helm.
    Beowulf addressed him    despite his baneful wound.
2725 He was well aware    that the world's pleasures,
days ere his death,    were now done for him,
earthly hours vanished,    the end approaching.
"Now I would give my son,    had I been granted one,
war-gear and weapons    to wield in battle,
2730 were there any heir    of my own body
remaining behind    for men to honor.
My folk I defended    for fifty years.
Neighboring nations    never had a leader
who would dare attack    with doughty allies,
2735 against me, menacing    with malice and warfare.
Thus on my lands I lived    my allotted time.
Well I warded    wealth and holdings,
kept not with quarrels    at the cost of deceit,
unrighteous oaths.    Yet this all I enjoyed,
2740 though I am sick and sad,    sorely wounded,

and when life leaves me    the lord need not blame me
for murder of kin.
                    "Most dear Wiglaf,
hurriedly hasten    to the hoard to see
the gold gathered there    under the gray boulder
2745  where the wounded wyrm    lies in unwaking sleep,
robbed of his riches.    Now run quickly
that I may surely see    the shining jewels,
ancient artwork,    objects of gold,
that I more peacefully    may depart from all—
2750  life, land, and home    that I long have held."
XXXVIII    Then they tell the tale    how trusty Wiglaf,
Wihstan's worthy son,    after the words spoken
at once obeyed Beowulf,    brave king of Geats
who lay weak from wounds    wearing his ringmail,
2755  braided battleshirt,    bowed 'neath the arches.
Then the fearless youth    by fortune gladdened
as he passed the ledge    saw precious gems,
gold glistening    on the ground ahead,
handsome hangings    and the home of the snake,
2760  dusk-flight dragon;    drinking-cups stood,
beakers of ancients,    without burnishers,
casings crumbling.    There were casques enough,
old and rusty,    arm-rings in plenty
cunningly coiled.    Costly treasure,
2765  earth-covered heirlooms,    easily conquer
all the human race,    hide it who wishes!
      Also hung on high    above the hoard there stood
a beautiful banner,    best of handiwork,
warp and woof of gold;    from it came a wondrous light
2770  so he could see objects    set on the pavement,
treasured artwork.    There was no trace at all
of the serpent there,    for the sword felled him.
I have heard that the hoard    hidden in the barrow
was sought and seized    by a single man,
2775  ancient artworks,    urns and goblets,
wealth as he wanted,    the war-standard too,
brightest banner.    The blade of the warlord
with its iron edge    had injured the keeper
of the gathered gold    who had guarded long

2780 by the hidden hoard    and sent hot terror
fiercely flaring    on the face of night
until it sank slaughtered    by the sword of steel.
  The herald hastened,    hoping to return
inspired by the splendor,    but spurred by questions
2785 whether he would meet alive    that manly spirit,
the prince of his people,    now deprived of strength
beside the stone arches    where he had stayed alone.
Then with that treasure    he returned finding
his belovèd lord    with his life ending,
2790 gory and bleeding.    Then he began gently
to wet him with water    until words burst through
to open utterance.
                            The agèd leader
gazed on the gold-hoard    and in grief he spoke:
"I give grateful thanks    to the glorious King,
2795 Leader eternal    and the Lord of all
for these ancient arms    that mine eyes behold,
because I may gather    for my good people
before my dying day    adornments so precious.
Now for this treasure-hoard    is my term of life
2800 finally bartered.    As for their further needs,
look to our people,    I can no longer stay.
Bid the battlefamed    build on the headland
a burial barrow,    bright from the embers.
It shall lift aloft    alone on Whale's Cape
2805 as a reminder there    to mine own people,
so that seafarers    will assign the name:
'Beowulf's Barrow'    when their broad vessels
drive from afar    over the darkening sea."
  Then the dauntless prince    drew from his neck
2810 a golden collar.    He gave his retainer,
the goodly guardian,    a gold-trimmed helmet,
curved torque and corslet,    bade him carry them well.
"You are the very last    to survive of us,
the Waymunding race.    Wilful fate sent
2815 all my dear kindred    to their destiny,
captains of courage.    I am called after."

Those were the final words    of the fallen king
before his funeral rites—    the flaming balefire,
blazing and burning.    From his breast there passed
2820  his spirit seeking    the splendor of the righteous.
[XXXIX]*    Then it went grievously    for the guiltless youth
that that dearest one    lay dying there,
in sore suffering.    His slayer likewise,
an awesome earthdragon    already slain,
2825  riven by ruin.    The ring-coiled serpent
no longer might lord it    over that load of wealth,
the buried bounty,    but the blade of steel,
hard hacked in war,    hammered and forged,
left it lifeless    so that the long serpent,
2830  far-flying snake,    fell to the hollow,
stilled by stabbing,    where stood the hoard.
Nevermore at night-time    in the nebulous air
could it circle above,    a sight for wonder,
boasting of its booty,    but to the bottom fell
2835  by the harsh handwork    of that hardy king.
Few freemen gained,    though they were firm in will,
forceful and fierce,    as the folk tell me,
or with daring deeds,    drove an onslaught
against the burning breath    of the beast's venom
2840  or rob the ringhall    with rude fingers,
if the defender were found.    Warlike Beowulf
paid the price of death    for the prized treasure.
Each had ended    the other's allotment
2845  of departing days.

                      After a pause to be sure;
his cowardly comrades    came from the forest,
trembling traitors,    ten together,
who had not dared before    to dart javelins
in their overlord's    utmost peril.
2850  But now shouldering shields,    shamefaced they came
armed for action,    where the old chief lay,
and they watched Wiglaf.    Wearily he sat there,
a loyal henchman    by his lord's shoulder
sprinkling springwater,    but it brought no spark of life.

2855 Well he wished it, but he could work no charm
to keep life in his lord nor yet lead aside
from God's purpose. It is He guides the deeds
of every being, Almighty One
in Whose care our course carries us home.
2860 Then speedily sprang from the respected youth
a cutting answer to those whose courage ebbed.
Wiglaf spoke out, Wihstan's offspring;
gloomy hearted he gazed at them.
"He who tells truly may talk of this,
2865 that the ruler of Geats who gave you rich treasure,
war-equipment, worn at this moment,
often offered along the alebenches
to henchmen here, helmets and breastmail,
the prince to his people, picking the most splendid
2870 that he found for friends both far and near,
and yet thus quickly he had cast away
those weeds for warriors when this war arrived.*
Not at all the country's king had any cause to boast
of his war-champions. Yet the World-ruler,
2875 God triumphant, granted him vengeance
singly with his swordblade when he sought valor.
Little could I offer in his life's defence,
yet in the close conflict as my kinsman's aid,
I surpassed my power in prior combats.
2880 When I drove my sword at the deadly foe,
it was ever weaker as its waning flames
flickered from it. Too few protectors
pressed round the prince at his passing hour.
Now must wealth-sharing and weapon-giving,
2885 delight in loved ones and land and home
fail for your families. Fellows of your kindred
must wander away wanting a landright
after foreign lords find out your deed,
failure and flight at the final attack;
2890 an infamous act. For every man
death is better than enduring shame!"

Then he had the outcome    of the action announced
      to the copse on the cliff    where that company
      of those men at arms    all the morning long
2895  sat sorrowing    foreseeing either
      that this day meant death    or the dear one's return.
      On horseback one hastened    to the headland's crest,
      nothing withholding    of the news of the fray,
      he spoke truthfully,    telling them all:
2900      "Now is our liberal lord,    leader of Weders,
      the defence of Geats,    fast on his deathbed.
      There he sleeps slaughtered    by the serpent's deed.
      Downed by daggers    his deadly opponent
      lies slain by his side.    No sword inflicted
2905  blow or blemish    on that beastly foe.
      The son of Wihstan    sits by Beowulf,
      Wiglaf the warrior,    one by the other,
      a heartweary guard    at their head keeps watch
      over loved and loathed,    lifeless together.
2910      "Now should our people    prepare for battle
      after Franks and Friesians    know the fall of our king,
      when it is broached abroad.    Bitter strife happened
      after Hygelac's host    came harrying
      with a fighting fleet    into Friesian lands
2915  where the Hetware    humbled him in battle,
      advancing with vigor    with vaster forces.
      The well-armed warrior,    wounded, succumbed
      among the foot-soldiers.    The fallen prince
      could dispense no spoils    to his special troop.
2920  We have never known    since that numbing loss
      Merovingian    mercy or kindness.
          "Nor can I promise    peace or loyalty
      from the Swedish folk,    for it is said abroad
      that that Ongentheow    ended the life
2925  of Hrethel's successor    near by Ravenswood,
      when first the Geats    fought with the Scylfings.
      At once that agèd king,    Ohthere's father,
      old and awesome,    made an onslaught there,
      retaliating,    trying for vengeance.

2930 He slew the sea king,  saved his consort,
now an old woman,  earlier his bride,
Onela's mother  and Ohthere's,
robbed of her riches.  He rushed to follow
until, though difficult,  they outdistanced him
2935 in Ravenswood,  bereft of their leader.
        "Then that huge army  hemmed in the remnant,
worn out by wounds.  He warned and threatened
the ill-omened troop  all night with bloodshed,
said that in morning light  he would mangle them,
2940 slashed by swordblows  or swinging on the gallows
as the bird's delight.  At the break of day
solace returned  to the sorrowful
when they heard the horn,  Hygelac's trumpet,
as that fine captain  followed his warriors
2945 with picked companions  from his experienced men.
XLI        "Then that trail of blood  was truly seen,
slaughter of soldiers,  Swedish and Geatish,
how the folk had waked  feuds and quarrels.
Then with his kinsmen  the kingly leader,
2950 sage and sorrowful,  sought the stronghold.
Then Ongentheow  turned off up a slope.
He had learned the hardihood  of Hygelac in warfare,
his pride and prowess;  to oppose the Geats,
defend his family  from fleets of war,
2955 and hold the hoard secure,  his heart misgave him.
Behind the earthen wall  the old king took cover.
Then they pursued the Swedes;  the sign of Hygelac,
the bright banners,  were there borne forward,
overrunning the refuge  as the Hrethling force
2960 came crowding on  toward the enclosed shelter.
There was Ongentheow,  old and grizzled,
indeed brought to bay  by the blades of swords,
so the gaunt ruler  must agree to all
willed by Eofor.  Wulf angrily
2965 slashed with his weapon,  sent blood spurting
beneath his faded hair.  The fearless Scylfing,
still undaunted,  straightway repaid
that stunning stroke  with a stronger blow
as he wheeled toward Wulf,  his weapon ready.

2970 Nor could the swift-handed    son of Wonred
      give the agèd king    answering fury,
      for he had hewed his head    through its helmet top;
      blood-stained, he tottered,    had to bow and fall.
      Yet he was not fated    and found his senses,
2975 although his wound rankled.    Before he wakened there.
      Eofor the Geat,    unyielding fighter,
      the hardy henchman,    Hygelac's retainer,
      cleft with his claymore    over the covering shields
      the high-crested helmet,    the headpiece from Sweden.
2980 Forged steel bit deep,    felled the Scylfing;
      the Swedish ruler    received his deathblow.
             "When the ground was cleared    and they had gained the
                                                field,
      many brought bindings    for the brother's wounds
      and rushed to raise him.    Meanwhile one robbed the dead,
2985 took from Ongentheow    his iron mailcoat,
      helm and hilted sword;    to Hygelac they brought it,
      arms and armor    of the agèd king.
      He took those trappings    and truly promised
      pay to the people;    plenty he gave them.
2990 When he was home again,    Hygelac's reward
      to Wulf and Eofor    was wealth unstinted.
      The warriors were awarded    to each the worth in rings
      of a hundred thousand    for their homes and lands—
      not one in the world of men    need at that reward reproach
                                                them;
2995 they had earned their honors    in that action in war.
      To Eofor was yielded    a young girl as bride,
      Hygelac's daughter,    the household jewel,
      as friendship token.
                          "That was the feud and war,
      malice of men,    that menace likely
3000 when Swedes discover    our sudden trouble—
      our lord lifeless,    who had led our troop
      against former foes,    and defended the coasts,
      the realm and its riches    against raids, defeat,
      threat of conquest,    theft and rapine.

3005 After defeat and fall    of former heroes
he worked for the welfare    of warriors of courage,*
and in all action    showed ideal conduct.
     "We must hasten now    to behold our prince
and on the path to the pyre    transport our lord,
3010 he who gave us gifts.    In the grip of flame
not just a single share    shall sink and vanish
with our valiant lord,    for there is vast treasure,
goldwork untold,    grimly purchased.
At the last his life    was lost for those riches.
3015 Then enfolded in flames    it must feed the pyre,
nor shall warrior wear    wealth as token,
nor lovely lady    light her beauty
with a twisted torque,    but treasures plundered,
aching-heartèd,    in alien lands
3020 they must wander wide    now the wise leader
laughs no longer,    leaves sport and joy.
Therefore must spearpoints spin,    speed cold at dawn,
hands hurling them;    not one harp will sound
to waken warriors,    as the wan raven
3025 dines on the doomed,    with dinning gabble
telling the eagle    of his tempting meal,
while with the ravening wolf    he rends the corpses."
     Thus the brave warrior    broached to his fellows
sorry tidings.    He did not deceive the troop
3030 with false facts or words.    The force all arose;
with an aching heart    toward Eagle headland
the men walked weeping    to that wondrous sight.
On the sand they saw,    his soul departed,
him who had granted gold    in those gladder days
3035 now here cold on his couch.    For the king of Geats
it was his parting day;    the prince of fighters,
great and good leader,    met a glorious death.
     They had stared before    at that strange creature,
the dread dragon there    by its den athwart;
3040 loathsome it lay,    a livid firedrake,
with its scaly skin    scorched by embers.

It was fifty feet    fully measured
lying at length.    Once it had loved flying
in the night aloft,    nearing again
3045    its den at dawning.    Death held it fast,
ended its holding    that earthcavern.
Bowls and beakers    abounded near them,
plates were lying    and precious swords,
riddled and rusty    as if they had rested there
3050    in the lap of earth    for a millennium.
Over that heaped up hoard,    huge and mighty,
all the golden gear    garnered of old,
charms had been chanted    so that no churl might reach
to that hall and hoard    unless heaven's Lord,
3055    true God of triumph,    Protector of warriors,
grant him whom He graces—    whoever seems good to Him—
the blessing of finding    and bringing out the treasure.
XLII        Then it was evident    the enterprise faltered
for him who hid within    those handsome jewels
3060    wrongly by the rampart.    Recently the dragon
felled one of a few,    but that fray was met
by violent vengeance.    Then in vain one seeks
where a courageous chief    may reach the end
of his allotted life,    when no longer now
3065    he keeps with his kinsmen    the court and meadhall.
So it was for Beowulf    when he met the barrow's guard,
in cruel conflict.    Beyond his ken to guess
how he must depart this plain,    pass from earth's duties.
So till the day of doom    damned solemnly
3070    by the great princes    who had garnered the hoard,
he who plundered the place    would be plunged in sin,
held in hellbonds    in a heathen cell
in terrible torment.    At no time before
had he taken closer count    of the costly gold
3075    that the owner left    in the arched cavern.
    Wiglaf spoke out,    Wihstan's successor:
"Often many men    have to submit to wrack
by one fixed purpose,    as has befallen us.
We could not counsel    the kingdom's ruler,

3080 belovèd leader,   with lore or reason
not to encounter   the keeper of the gold-hoard,
but to let him lie   where he long had been,
frequenting the cavern   to the close of the world.
He held to his high cause.   The hoard has been examined
3085 that he so grimly gained.   Too great was the power
that impelled thither   the people's ruler.
I was inside there   and have seen it all,
the cave's costly holdings,   when it was cleared for me
and a lane allowed,   not lightly granted,
3090 in under the earthwall.   Eagerly I gathered
a huge heap of stores,   of hoarded treasure,
carried quickly   to my king hither.
He was still living,   alert and conscious.
In his pain he spoke   plainly, fully,
3095 and gave you greeting.   The grand old hero
bade you build up,   where the balefire stood,
a memorial mound,   massive and splendid,
to honor his exploits   as of all the men
he had the most merit   on the mighty earth,
3100 while he might secure and keep   the court and treasure.
      "Let us now hasten   to behold again
that crowded cluster   of curious jewels,
strange stores that lie   beneath the stony cliff.
I shall guide to the gold.   You will see gear enough,
3105 bracelets and breastmail.   Get the bier ready,
prepare it promptly.   When we appear again
we shall carry our king,   our kindly leader,
where he long must lie   in the Lord's keeping."
      Then the warhero,   Wiglaf, ordered
3110 many of the fightingmen,   faithful comrades,
who were householders,   that they heap up wood,
fetchèd from afar,   for the folk chieftain,
for their hero-king.   "Now must heat devour
the prince of the people,   their precious captain,—
3115 the dying flames darken—   him who had dared the storm
of arrows arching,   iron showers,
withstanding staunchly   the stream of missiles
that flew at the phalanx,   flight successful
as the feathered shaft   furthered the barb."

3120    Thus the sensible    son of Wihstan
       called from the cadre    of the king's guardsmen
       a peerless seven,    picked as finest,
       he, the eighth warrior,    led under the evil roof;
       first at the forefront    one bore a flaming brand.
3125   It was not left to lot    who should loot the hoard;
       where soldiers sighted    in the sunken hall
       unguarded objects    of any value
       left lying there,    with little worry
       they quickly carried    the costly treasures
3130   out from the earthcave.    To the edge of the cliff
       they dragged the dragon;    down he tumbled
       for the flood to enfold    in the furrowed wave.
       Then was twisted gold    tossed on wagons,
       untold objects.    The agèd warrior,
3135   their king, was carried    to the Cape of Whales.
XLIII       Then the people, the Geats,    prepared for their chieftain
       an imposing pyre    at the planned gravesite,
       hung with helmets,    hard battleshields,
       bright breastarmor    as he had bidden them.
3140   In the midst they laid    the mighty leader,
       guardsmen grieving    for their gallant chief.
       They began to kindle    on the cliff-barrow
       a most furious fire    fueled by driftwood.
       Smoke swirled aloft    in swelling cloudplumes,
3145   black over burning,    the blaze roaring,
       mingled with mourning;    moan of winds stilled
       until the body burst    in the brutal heat,
       hot at the heart's core.    Unhappy of spirit,
       they grieved at that great loss,    their good ruler's death.
3150   The Weder woman*    with wound coils of hair,
       mourned lamenting    mighty Beowulf
       in sorrowful song,    sadly repeating
       that ravage and ruin,    arrest and abasement
       were her deepest dread    in days of grieving
3155   at the horror of hosts.    Heaven drank the smoke.
           Then the Weder-Geats    worked to fashion
       a hillock on the headland.    It was high and broad,
       widely apparent    to all wanderers,

and in ten days' time    a tomb was ready
3160   for the war-famous king.    They walled his ashes,
rimmed with a rampart    most regally splendid,
as was designed and planned    by discerning men.
They placed in the barrow    bracelets and neck-rings,
all such ornaments    as were earlier
3165   hauled from the hoard    by hostile warriors.
What the lords had left    they relinquished to earth,
all that gold in the ground    that guards it still,
as useless as of yore    to youths or elders.
      Then around the barrow    brave warriors rode,
3170   children of chieftains,    champions all twelve.
They wished to bewail    their woe, lamenting
the king with keening,    acclaimed his lordship
and his worthy works,    well done, courageous,
that they deemed doughty.    Thus it is duly just
3175   that one praise his prince    in poem and story
and hold him in heart    when he must head away
forth from flesh elsewhere.    Thus his fellow Geats,
chosen champions    cheerlessly grieved
for the loss of their lord,    leader and defender.
3180   They called him of captains,    kings of the known world,
of men most generous    and most gracious,
kindest to his clansmen,    questing for praise.*

18. Beow: The ms. has *Beowulf*, which seems to be due to confusion with the subject of the poem. Beow in the genealogies is given as the son of Scyld. Both are early nature deities. See also line 53.

19. Ms. *Scedeland*, modern Skåne, the southernmost part of Sweden. In 1686 ms. *Scedenig*, there translated "Scylding country," that is, Danish country, which at the time it was.

53. *I* indicates beginning of first fitt. These roman numerals appear in the ms.

62. [Yrsa] is from Norse sources, not in ms., and her husband's name there is *-ela*. No further mention of Hrothgar's sister occurs, but Onela plays more than a negligible role in the poem.

389–390, 403. Bracketed half-lines not in ms. I translate Klaeber's emendation.

586. The ms. lacks alliteration in this line. I have assumed that *fagum*, a frequent epithet for a sword (glossed in its many uses here as "shining; stained; blood-stained; variegated," none of these appropriate here) was written for a less usual word *incrum*, "of you two," as in line 584, "neither of you two." This supplies vowel alliteration with *ic*, "I," in the head stave, and both with contrasted stress.

769. "End of alefeasts": ms. *caluscerwen*. This is a well-known crux. Two meanings have been proposed: "dispensing of ale" or the "deprival of ale" depending on which verb had *-scerwen* as its noun form. Since the Danes are terrified by the sounds of the battle between Beowulf and Grendel that is shaking the great hall of Hart to its foundations, they expect the worst for it—deprivation of ale, which in the runic inscriptions of Scandinavia is the magic word *alu*, meaning "ale" or "protection" or "luck." What could be worse for a banquet-hall?

1850–1851. The ms. irregularly marks length; therefore, it is impossible to tell whether þe represents "thee," dative of comparison, or a reduced form of "that." I have translated it "you," the modern equivalent of "thee." For a discussion of the matter, see the ASPR (Anglo-Saxon Poetic Records) notes to *Beowulf*, vol. 4.

1950. "Furrowed flood": The ms. reads *ofer fealone flod*. In the Middle Ages many peoples worried less about differences in hue than we do now; still, "fallow," used of sandy paths, horses, and ploughed fields and often translated "yellow," is a very earthy color for the sea. Its use as the color of ploughed land goes back to its derivation from *fealh*, "a plough" or "the rim of a wheel," "felly." It is no long step from "fallow," "ploughed" to "furrowed," which seems appropriate for the North Sea.

2164. "Dappled bays": The ms. *æppelfealuwe*, "applefallow," is a compound of *fealu* of the preceding note. In metalwork "apple" is used for beading, decorating with round studs, and for a boss as on a shield. "Dapple" is probably derived from, perhaps blended with Norse *depill*, which also means "spotted" or "a spot." Where we would say "dapple gray," Chaucer, describing the Reeve's horse Stot or Scot says "pomely grey," using a French derivative from *pomme*, "apple." Spotted horses were conspicuous and preferred for that, acquiring a reputation as fast, reliable, and of unusual stamina. The Palouse Indians of Idaho and Washington learned the principles of horse-breeding from Spaniards, but assumed the color was the object of the breeding and developed the Appaloosa, a horse that the cowboys came to respect for its other qualities.

2189. The young Geats who despised Beowulf were probably his uncles, Herebald and Hathcyn; perhaps too, Hygelac at that age, unless he was more likely to take his father's attitude. Hrethel had fetched Beowulf from his daughter's house when he was only seven years old, and Hygelac may have been no more than ten. One reason for accepting the sister's (in this instance, the daughter's) son was that one's own sons had a claim on the throne and were more of a threat. Hygelac became king after

the deaths of Hrethel, Herebald, and Hathcyn, and
Beowulf accepts the kingship only after Hygelac's son,
Heardred, is killed.

2341.  "Faring from daylight": The ms. is brittle and broken
here so that we have only *þend daga*. Many editors
emend to *lændaga*, "loan of days" because it makes some
sense and occurs in line 2591. Kemp Malone supplied
*liþend*. But Beowulf is now defending his own country
and the emendation would refer to him as a voyager. I
propose *beliþend* which would mean one who is passing
away, dying, confirming the king's earlier premonition.
The ms. could easily accommodate those four letters in
the preceding line.

2360–2361.  Even for the hero this seems an incredible feat and
has been given more comment than it really needs.
We have read that Beowulf has the strength of thirty
men (379–381), and of his swimming exploit with Breca,
his underwater fight against Grendel's mother, and
exaggerated numbers of years. Numbers are conventional
and if we accept that history does not mention Beowulf
and that he fights with both trolls and dragons, we need
scarcely balk at exaggerated details.

2821.  Fitt number not in ms.

2865–2872.  When a young soldier was selected to serve his lord,
especially among the loyal and experienced followers
or henchmen, his chief gave him weapons and armor.
Wiglaf feels those gifts were wasted on these cowards,
who did not go to their king's aid when he most needed
them. Compare with their conduct Beowulf's and the
gifts that Hrothgar gave him which he gave to his king
on his return from Denmark. Another aspect of rewards
was to recognize exploits beyond the line of duty,
obligations of the most devoted followers to their lord
and his to them. Hygelac is even more generous to
Beowulf than Hrothgar.

3006.  The ms. has *scyldingas*, but it was only defending Hart
Hall that Beowulf served the Danes—as far as we know.
*Scylfingas*, the Swedish people apparently related to
Beowulf through his father, have been suggested as

an emendation and more recently *scildwigan,* "shield-warriors." This could include all these peoples and the Geats.

3150.  It has been suggested that "the Weder woman" whose prominence at the funeral would suggest that she might be the widow could well be Hygd. In early times the right to the kingdom was often thought to reside in the wife of the rightful king. Beowulf is not in the direct line of succession. This importance of the dead king's widow may lie behind the story of Oedipus's marriage to his mother Jocasta after he killed his father, not recognizing either parent. Certainly Hygd asked the hero to take over the kingdom when he returns home after killing Dayraven, Hygelac's slayer. But Beowulf offers rather to protect her boy until he is old enough to reign and only accepts the throne (and perhaps her hand) after Heardred has been killed in the Swedish wars.

3182.  Ms. *lofgearnost.* Literally this means "most eager for praise." Politicians, however, have often demonstrated that the most eager are often the most unscrupulous. The meaning is rather to bear in mind the imminence of death and so do nothing to tarnish one's name. Notice that true to those prechristian times, the hero is not looking to the bliss of God's favor, but how men regard him. I translate "questing" to stress that he has worked constantly toward that end.

# Appendix:
# The Finnsburg Fragment

Compare Beowulf 1066–1159.
*These two sources tell us all we know of this confrontation.*

Hnæf Hocing and the Danes hold off the Friesians
in the great hall of Finnsburg.

". . . Gables are burning!"
Hnæf, new to strife   announced his answer:
"Day is not dawning   nor dragon soaring,
nor here in this hall   high gables burn,
5   but now they bear forward.   Birds are calling,
war-spears whining,   and wolves howling;
shield answers shaft.   Shining moonlight
wanders over wasteland.   Wicked deeds arise
that will form hatred   in this force's heart.
10   But awaken now,   warriors of mine;
take up your targes,   determine on courage,
fight at the forefront,   be firm in valor."
    Gold-studded thanes   girded on broadswords.
To the doors they dashed,   daring fighters,
15   Sigeferth and Eaha,   their swords in hand,
and at the other door   Ordlaf and Guthlaf,
and behind hastened   Hengest himself.
Then still Garulf   urged Guthhere
not to venture assault   and his so valued life
20   at the first onset   on Finnsburg's hall
now the savage foe   sought to take it.
Above the crowd he called,   clearly, boldly,
demanding to know   who manned the door.
"Sigeferth, my name,   a Secgan chieftain,
25   a well-known wanderer.   Wars and hardships
have I found in full.   You may find here now
whichever you will get from me:   good or evil."
    Then was heard in the hall   the havoc of slaughter;
champions shouldered   their enchased shieldguards;
30   horned helmets burst;   the hallfloor pounded
until Garulf sank   in that grim battle,

first fightingman   to fall of any,
son of Guthlaf—   around him soldiers of worth,
the restless now corpses.   The raven circled,
35  swarthy, sallowbrown.   Swords flashed alight
as if all Finnsborough   were a flaring blaze.
I never heard of worthier   in warfare than those,
sixty soldiers   serving their chief,
and of no payment given   for the pale mead-drink
40  like that this troop of Hnæf's   returned their leader.
Five days they fought   so there fell not one
of the hall comrades,   but they held the doors.

   Then a wounded youth   went from the conflict,
said that his breastmail   was broken and torn,
45  hauberk worthless   and his helmet pierced.
Then the people's prince   plied him with questions
how these warriors fared,   wounded in combat,
or which young soldiers . . .

# Annotated Index
## of Proper Names

Abel: Biblical character, son of Adam. 108

Alfhere: kinsman of Wiglaf, conjectured to be the original Beowulf, probably because his name alliterates with Ecgtheow. It is generally thought that Beowulf (the bee-wolf, or bear) is a nickname, for his bearlike strength. 2604

Ashhere: favored thane and counselor of Hrothgar. 1323, 1329, 1420, 2123

Beanstan: father of Breca. 524

Beow: son of Scyld. 18 (see note), 53

Beowulf: the hero, son of Ecgtheow the Waymunding, a Swedish tribe; a Geat, sister's son to Hygelac; later himself king of the Geats. Passim throughout

Breca: son of Beanstan, chief of the Brondings; as boys he and Beowulf had a swimming contest. 506, 531, 583

Brondings: unidentified tribal name. 520

Brosing (probably more correctly Brising): a race of dwarves who made a magic necklace for the Norse goddess Freya; it was later lost. 1199

Cain: brother of Abel (see Genesis iv). 107, 1261

Dane, Danes: (also any compounds for alliteration North-, South-, etc.). 117–2495 passim

Dayraven: slayer of Hygelac who had invaded the Frankish territory; slain by Beowulf. 2501

Denmark: at the time of the poem the island of Zealand, on which is modern Copenhagen, and the southern province, Skåne, of Sweden. It was surrounded by other Germanic tribes. 3, 384, 394, 463, 465, 1417, 2124

Eadgils: Swedish prince, son of Ohthere and brother of Eanmund; they are exiled from Sweden by their uncle Onela for rebellion, and received by Heardred, Hygelac's son. When Onela invades Geatland for vengeance on the rebel princes, Heardred is killed. Beowulf succeeds him as the King of Geats and later helps Eadgils slay Onela and take the Swedish throne. 2392.

Eaha: Danish warrior. FF 15

Eanmund: Swedish prince, son of Ohthere and brother of Eadgils. 2611, 2617.

Ecglaf: father of Unferth the Dane. 499, 590, 980, 1465, 1808

Ecgtheow: father of Beowulf; a Waymunding (a Swedish family); marries the only daughter of Hrethel the Geatish king; slays the Wylfing (a Germanic family), Heatholaf; he escapes to Denmark and Hrothgar pays his *wergild*. 263, 373, 529, 631, 957, 1383, 1473, 1550, 1651, 1817, 1999, 2177, 2366, 2399, 2425, 2587

Ecgwela: a Danish king, known only from this poem. 1710

Eofor: Geatish warrior, son of Wonred and brother of Wulf; slayer of the Swedish king Ongentheow, and rewarded with marriage to Hygelac's daughter. 2486, 2964, 2976, 2991, 2996

Eomer: Anglian prince, son of Offa, grandson of Garmund, and kinsman of Hemming. 1960

Eormenric: a powerful Ostrogothic king of the later fourth century. 1201

Finn: king of the East Friesians and also the Jutes; son of Folcwalda; married to Hildeburh, a Halfdane. 1081, 1096, 1116, 1129, 1137, 1146, 1152, 1157

Finnsburg: Finn's capital in Friesland. FF 20, Finnsborough 36

Fitela: son and nephew of Sigemund, the dragon-slayer. 879, 889

Folcwalda: father of Finn, the Friesian. 1090

Franks: a Germanic tribe of the Rhine Valley, 1210, 2502, 2911

Freawaru: daughter of Hrothgar; married Ingeld of the Heathobards, apparently to keep peace between his people and the Danes. 2022

Friesians/Frisians: a Germanic tribe. Its language is closer to English than other Low German dialects. 1069, 1093, 1104, 1206, 2359, 2503, 2911, 2914

Friesland: land of the Friesians. In the East, Finn's kingdom; in the West, allied with the Franks against Hygelac. 1125

Garmund: father of the Anglian king Offa. 1962

Garulf: a Friesian. FF 18, 31

Geats: a tribe in southeast Sweden, Beowulf's people. 194–3177 passim

Gifthas: East Germanic people. 2495

Grendel: a monster of the marshes. 102–2521 passim

Guthhere: a Friesian. FF 18

Guthlaf: a Dane. 1148, FF 16

Guthlaf: a Friesian. FF 33

Haereth: father of Hygd. 1928, 1980

Halfdane: king of Danes, son of Beow, father of Hrothgar. 56, 189, 268, 344, 468, 645, 1009, 1020, 1039, 1064, 1474, 1652, 1698, 1866, 2011, 2142, 2147

Halfdanes: the Danish tribe that Hoc, Hnaef, and Hildeburh belonged to. 1068

Hama: early Germanic figure, probably a Goth. 1198

Handscioh: a Geat who follows Beowulf to Denmark; the first killed by Grendel. 2076

Hart/Heorot: the great banquet-hall that Hrothgar has built after he becomes King of Denmark. 78–2115 passim

Hathcyn: second son of Hrethel; he accidentally shoots his brother. 2434, 2437, 2483

Heardred: son of Hygelac, killed in the Swedish wars. 2201, 2374, 2381, 2388

Heathobard: a Germanic tribe, their king Ingeld. 2032, 2037, 2067

Heatholaf: an East Germanic Wylfing slain by Ecgtheow. 460

Helga: Hrothgar's younger brother. 61

Helmings: the tribe from which Wealhtheow came. 620

Hemming: an Angle, kinsman of Offa and Eomer. 1944, 1961

Hengest: an officer of the Halfdanes who succeeded Hnaef to leadership. 1082, 1091, 1096, 1127, FF 17

Heorot: See Hart/Heorot

Herebald: Hrethel's eldest son, killed by Hathcyn. 2434, 2464

Heregar: son of Halfdane and elder brother of Hrothgar. 61, 467, 2158

Heremod: Danish king, killed by the Jutes; a bad ruler. 904, 915, 1709

Hereric: uncle of Heardred, brother of Hygd. 2206

Hereward: Heregar's son, but passed over for the kingship. 2161

Hetware: the Chattuarii, close to the Franks of the Lower Rhine. 2362, 2915

Hildeburh: Finn's Queen of Friesland, daughter of Hoc the Half-dane, sister of Hnaef. 1071, 1114

Hnaef: leader of the Halfdanes, killed at Finnsburg by the Friesians. 1068, FF 2, 40

Hoc: king of Halfdanes, father of Hnaef and Hildeburh. 1077

Hreosnabeorh: "Mare's Hill," site of a battle between the Geats and Swedes. 2478

Hrethel: king of the Geats; father of Hygelac; Beowulf's maternal grandfather. 374, 454, 1484, 2191, 2387, 2430, 2474, 2928

Hrethling: Hrethel's son (Hygelac) or the followers of Hrethel (Geats). 2959

Hrethric: elder son of Hrothgar and Wealhtheow. 1189, 1836

Hrothgar: Danish king, son of Halfdane; builder of Hart Hall. 61-2155 passim

Hrothmund: younger son of Hrothgar and Wealhtheow. 1189

Hrothulf: son of Helga and co-ruler with Hrothgar of the Danes. For a more historical account of events only hinted at in the poem, see Chambers' *Beowulf: An Introduction*. 1015, 1180

Hrunting: Unferth's famous sword, loaned to Beowulf. 1457, 1490, 1660, 1807

Hunlafing: son(s) of Hunlaf (Guthlaf and Oslaf [1148]?). 1143

Hygd: Hygelac's Queen, daughter of Haereth, mother of Heardred, possibly Beowulf's widow. 1925, 2173, 2369

Hygelac: king of the Geats, maternal uncle of Beowulf. 194-2997 passim

Ingeld: son of Froda, king of the Heathobards; marries Freawaru, Hrothgar's daughter. 2025, 2065

Jutes: followers of Finn and the Friesians. 903, 1072, 1088, 1141, 1145

Lappish shore (ms. Finnaland): probably not Finland or Finnmark in northern Scandinavia, but perhaps Finnheden in Sweden. (See also the note to line 2360.) 580

Merovingian: of the Franks. 2921

Naegling: Beowulf's sword, taken from Dayraven. 2680

Offa: king of the Continental Angles. 1951, 1958

Ohthere: elder son of Ongentheow, king of Sweden; father of
Eanmund and Eadgils; brother of Onela. 2380, 2394,
2611, 2927, 2932

Onela: younger son of Ongentheow, the Swedish king;
marries Hrothgar's sister; killed by Eadgils. 62, 2387,
2616, 2932

Ongentheow: Swedish king, father of Ohthere and Onela; slain by
Eofor, a Geat. 1967, 2387, 2475, 2486, 2924, 2951,
2961, 2985

Ordlaf: a Dane. FF 16

Oslaf: follower of Hnaef and Hengest (perhaps the same
as Ordlaf, due to r/s confusion in the Insular ms.
hand). 1148

Ravenswood: Swedish forest where Ongentheow killed Hathcyn,
brother of Hygelac the Geat. 2925, 2935

Reams: Scandinavian tribe from territory of southeast Norway in Romerike. 519

Scefing: Scyld's epithet, meaning son of "Sheaf" or with a
sheaf. 4

Scyld: mythical Danish king. 4, 19, 26

Scylding: a descendant or follower of Scyld, that is, a Dane.
30–2159 passim

Scylfing: Swedish royal family, in the plural the Swedes;
meaning "of the shelving rock." 63, 2383, 2487, 2603,
2926, 2966, 2980

Secgan: Germanic coastal tribe. FF 24

Sigeferth: a Secgan, one of Hnaef's fighters. FF 15, 24

Sigemund: son of Waels; father and uncle of Fitela. 875, 884

Sweden: territory north of Denmark and Germany, east of
Norway. 19, 2495, 2979

Swerting: maternal uncle or maternal grandfather of Hygelac. 1202

Thryth: wife of the Anglian king Offa. 1930

Unferth: spokesman and trusted adviser to Hrothgar, but
with a shady past. 499, 530, 1165, 1456, 1465, 1488

Waelsing: son of Waels, that is Sigemund. 877, 895

Waymunding: Chambers identifies this as a Swedish tribe; Beowulf
and Wiglaf were of this family. 2607, 2814

Wealhtheow: Hrothgar's Queen. 612, 629, 664, 1162, 1215, 2173

Weder: "storm-loving"; at first an epithet of the seafaring

Geats, used in poetry as an alternative name for
them. 224–3156 passim

Weland: superhuman smith and armorer of Germanic legend. 455

Wendels: a Scandinavian tribe, Vandals, who have left their
name on lands in Sweden and northern Jutland. 348

Whale's Cape: translation of Hronesnaes, where Beowulf was buried. 2804, 3135

Wiglaf: the last Waymunding, son of Wihstan; kinsman and
most loyal follower of Beowulf. 2602, 2631, 2720,
2742, 2751, 2852, 2862, 2907, 3076, 3109

Wihstan: father of Wiglaf; fought for Onela against the Geats
and slew Ohthere's son Eanmund. 2602, 2613, 2752,
2862, 2906, 3076, 3120

Withergyld: Heathobard warrior. 2052

Wonred: a Geat, father of Eofor and Wulf. 2970

Wulf: son of Wonred; fights Ongentheow. 2964, 2969, 2991

Wulfgar: prince of the Wendels (Vandals), an officer in
Hrothgar's court. 348, 359

Wylfing: Germanic tribe on the south Baltic coast. 461, 471

Yrmenlaf: a Dane, younger brother of Ashhere. 1324

Yrsa: daughter of Halfdane, sister of Hrothgar; marries
Onela. 62

# Genealogies of the
# Royal Families

## THE DANES

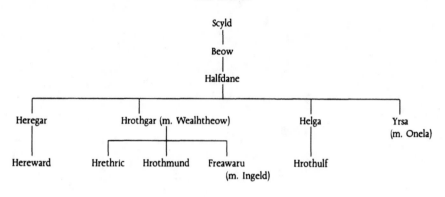

Scyld
|
Beow
|
Halfdane

Heregar — Hrothgar (m. Wealhtheow) — Helga — Yrsa (m. Onela)

Hereward — Hrethric — Hrothmund — Freawaru (m. Ingeld) — Hrothulf

## THE GEATS

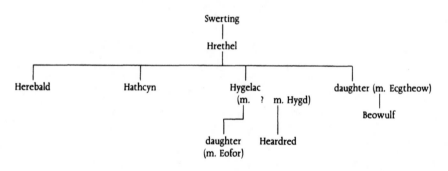

Swerting
|
Hrethel

Herebald — Hathcyn — Hygelac (m. ? m. Hygd) — daughter (m. Ecgtheow)

daughter (m. Eofor) — Heardred — Beowulf

## THE SWEDES

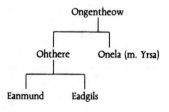

Ongentheow

Ohthere — Onela (m. Yrsa)

Eanmund — Eadgils